GENESIS

A DELIGHT MINISTRIES STUDY

Bap of 29
Help pass out finals stuff

DELIGHT MINISTRIES

Delight Ministries
www.delightministries.com

Printed in the United States of America
First Printing: January 2022
Believers Press
ISBN: 978-1-7343272-3-6

OUR MISSION

Our mission is to invite college women into **Christ-centered community** that **fosters vulnerability** and **transforms stories.**

Christ-Centered Community

We launch, grow, and sustain thriving Christ-centered communities on college campuses. We've seen time and time again that community is often the catalyst for true Kingdom impact.

Foster Vulnerability

We aim to provide a space on college campuses for women to vulnerably share how Christ has been at work in their lives. We believe that vulnerability leads to breakthrough, and breakthrough leads to transformation!

Transforms Stories

We believe that one moment with Jesus can truly change everything. Our mission is to give college women numerous opportunities to meet with Jesus and have their lives transformed!

HOW TO READ THIS BOOK

We like to think of this Genesis book as a "choose your own adventure." We want you to move at your own pace, studying as much or as little as you want. There are three basic routes you can take as you navigate this study:

ALL-IN GENESIS NERD

Option 1 is for the girl who is ready to lock in and fully study the book of Genesis. This means interacting with every page of the book, including reading every chapter of Genesis, taking your own notes, reviewing with our summaries, and diving into the main teaching for the week already armed with context, background, and prayer. This option will give you the fullest understanding of the overarching narrative of the book of Genesis as a whole.

 ## SUMMARY QUEEN

Option 2 is for the girl who really wants to make the most of this Genesis study but doesn't have much extra time in her schedule for extensive reading. If you're this girl, you'll use the chapter summaries we provide to your advantage, reading through them to get a general understanding of the context but skipping the notes section and opening your Bible straight to the verses that week's teaching covers.

Option 3 is for the girl who just wants to be ready to join the conversation at her Delight chapter that week. Maybe you're crazy busy with school or are going through a different book in your quiet time, so you want to stick to what you need to know to be prepared for Delight every week. Your best option in this scenario will be to skip the summary and notes pages all together, diving straight into that week's teaching after prayer.

Whichever option you choose is a great option! Remember, the word of God is active and never returns void. Whether you read a lot or a little, you'll still be blessed and you'll still get to know the character of your God in a new, deeper way.

Now let's take a closer look at the different parts of this study!

Each week of our study covers five chapters of Genesis. At the beginning of each week you will find summaries of each chapter. Whether you use them for review or as a context aid, these summaries are helpful in giving you a full picture of the overarching narrative of Genesis.

NOTES

In addition to the summaries, each week contains a notes section that's useful for jotting down notes as you read your Bible, verses you loved that you want to discuss with your chapter, or even things you heard in your weekly gathering that you want to remember. Cover this page with words and doodles or leave it empty. It's up to you!

PRAY THIS PRAYER!

We would be silly to try to study the word of God without inviting His Holy Spirit to be a part of it. By praying before you study, you are allowing God to fill you, giving you deeper understanding and conviction where you need it. Don't skip this step! It's crucial! We've prepared prayers for you in advance, but feel free to just take this section as a reminder to talk to the Lord about what He is stirring in your heart.

MAIN TEACHING

Every week of our study zooms in on a specific moment in Scripture. We walk you through the Scripture with helpful tools like:

+ **Read this**

+ **Fill in the Blank** _____

+ **Question Box** [   ]

+ **HARD TRUTH TIME!**

We encourage you to dive into these sections, answering every prompt and reading the Scripture highlighted in grey. You would be surprised by how easy it is to do a Bible study without ever actually opening your Bible! Interacting with this study as thoroughly as you can will help you prepare for vulnerable conversation in your Delight weekly gathering.

TIPS FOR READING SCRIPTURE

The truth is: reading Scripture isn't always easy! It's a muscle that you have to stretch and grow over time. I've compiled a list of tips from some of my friends that I think will help you to start to love your daily time in the Word. These are all practical tips that will help you to better hear the voice of God through the Scripture.

#1 Prepare Your Heart – This is SO simple! Every day before you open the Word, ask God to simply prepare your heart, show up, and speak to you. Reading the Bible isn't something we have to do on our own or through our own power. The Word is alive—meaning that God can and will speak to you through it. All you have to do is ask!

#2 Ask Good Questions – This can seriously change the way you encounter the Bible! The best tool we have to understand the word of God is our own ability to ask the right questions. If you've ever read Scripture and not understood something (a.k.a. me every day of my life) . . . that's an invitation to ask a question. What? When? How? Where? Who? Why? Dig into your questions and seek out answers!

For some of your more historical or practical questions, you can read Biblical commentaries, get a Study Bible, or talk to someone who knows more than you. For the other more complex questions, bring them to the feet of Jesus and simply ask. He cares and can provide answers in some of the coolest ways! This isn't your college calculus class where you have to be afraid to ask in the fear of looking stupid. There is a loving, caring, and gentle Father on the other end of the line ready to dialogue with you.

*If this is new to you . . . don't worry! We're going to ask A LOT of questions of the text together in this book.

#3 Read it at Your Own Pace – Take your time with reading Scripture! You have your entire life to read the Bible. If you want to mediate on one verse for an entire week—do it! If you want to read the entire Bible in a month—do that, too! Go at the pace that feels comfortable to you. Don't be afraid to slow down and dive really deep in certain parts when you feel led to.

#4 Talk About What You're Learning – Some of the best moments of revelation from Scripture happen by simply talking to the people around you about the things you've been reading. This isn't a journey you have to travel alone! Be sure to talk about how God is speaking to you through His Word with your roommate, friends, parents, and your Delight community!

#5 Follow the Spirit – When you're reading your Bible, don't be afraid to change course from where you initially started. You may start out reading Genesis, but then feel a nudge to re-read that Psalm you heard the other day. Don't ignore those nudges! When you open up your heart to hear from the Lord, He may redirect you to another passage of Scripture. That is absolutely okay. You never know what He might be leading you to.

TABLE OF CONTENTS

BEFORE WE BEGIN

In elementary school, I attended a private Lutheran school. I remember the playground, the uniforms, and that one time I got sent to the principal's office (only to pick up another student, obviously). But one thing I remember with even more clarity was the huge mural on the wall outside of my Spanish class. I'm pretty sure the whole hall was filled with these paintings—all depictions of famous Bible stories—but I couldn't tell you what the rest of them were. For some reason, I can only remember the art right outside Señora Novak's room.

It was the sacrifice of Isaac.

I remember staring up at it every day. Teenage Isaac was lying on a rock while his father Abraham stood over him with a knife. It was almost gruesome, the looks on their faces and the sharpness of the weapon meant to kill. But in the background, hidden in the bushes, I could see the ram that the Lord had sent as the substitute sacrifice. It was a still life, a haunting rendering of a moment that could have gone either way.

I'm not sure why that image is burned into my mind. I've read the book of Genesis countless times; it was my starting point for mandatory Bible reading time in school. Each time, I started at Genesis and committed to trying to read the whole Bible—all sixty-six books—in our thirty minute windows. Little Maggie was just as competitive then as I am now, maybe too much.

All that to say, I knew the stories of the Bible. I knew the stories of Genesis like they were my own memories. I had dressed up as Eve for halloween, and I played Noah and the Ark with my friends at recess. So why was I so consumed with that picture of Isaac and Abraham?

I wonder if, subconsciously, it bothered me. Why in the world would a school for children be displaying child sacrifice on the walls? Why were we so blatantly celebrating one of the darker moments of the Bible? I had spent so much time in Genesis and Exodus during those early years of my faith that it shouldn't have been shocking. I knew that God was big, powerful, and allowed to do whatever He wanted. That's what I had learned, studied, and heard from all of my teachers and pastors.

But that same powerful God had made Himself personal to me. In maybe 3rd or 4th grade I had a dream. Or I guess it wasn't a dream. It was God interrupting my dream to tell me something. I had been dreaming about something else when it suddenly went black, and I heard God say, "Maggie, it's time to wake up." I obediently opened my eyes and saw that my alarm hadn't gone off; if I didn't get up right then, I was going to be late to school.

For years I ran around telling everyone who would listen that *God* had woken me up for school! It felt so cool, so intimate. I knew that He cared enough about me to know that I wouldn't want to be late. He was a God who was involved in the little details of my life, a God who cared about what I cared about.

I think younger me had trouble reconciling the idea of that personal, caring God with the God on the mural who told Abraham to kill his own son. That trouble must haunt me even now, all these years later, because here I am, writing a book about Genesis and the character of God.

And I think maybe that same thing is haunting you, too.

We want to know God. The fact that you even picked up this book proves that you have some inkling to learn more about your Creator, to get closer to Him, or to try to be more like Him.

But it's so hard to become familiar with the character of God when He is so multifaceted and when there are some parts of His character that seem to contradict each other.

How can God be big *and* personal?

How can God be merciful *and* deliver punishment?

How can God be good *and* still allow bad things to happen?

We are all a little bit "God confused." We like to hold on too tightly to one aspect of His character and totally miss another. Or we completely give up on trying to understand Him and just say, "Oh well, I guess I'll never know." But I don't think we are called to settle. The beautiful thing about a life with God is the growth that comes with it!

In Philippians, Paul says that he prays, "that your love may abound more and more in knowledge and depth of insight" (Philippians 1:9). We are allowed to take baby steps! We are allowed to fall more in love with God every day, and He *wants* us to seek Him! He wants us to learn His heart!

I wish I could go back and tell younger Maggie to take a closer look at that mural. I wish I could tell her that she was focusing on the wrong part. She would have seen that ram hidden in the bushes and seen the tender mercy of a God who will always provide. That ram hidden in the bushes was a sign of the same God who woke her up for school that day.

God is so much bigger than any box you could put Him in. Looking back, I don't even think God just wanted to wake me up for school that day. I think He was telling me to *wake up* and see Him. I think that was when He called me to serve Him and follow Him for all of my life. I am so thankful for a God who can be everything I need and still have more to give.

It is vital to know the character of God. It's more vital than breathing or a steady heartbeat. Why? Because life is hard, and when things go downhill, we need to know who we can rely on. God is our solid rock. We need to know who He is and what He stands for. Then when trials come our way, we will not stumble.

Because we have a good God who's got our back.

Do you know Him like that? It's okay if you don't yet! My prayer for you as you study the book of Genesis is that you would begin to trust the character of your Creator. Then when He calls you, you'll be ready.

Let's encounter His heart together.

XOXO,
Maggie Sawler
DELIGHT MINISTRIES
CURRICULUM DEVELOPMENT COORDINATOR

CHAPTER 1

GOD BREATHES LIFE

GENESIS
CHAPTERS 1-5

Switch your Crocs to sport mode, because we are SPRINTING into our ten week, deep-dive study of the (literally) groundbreaking book of Genesis. Go ahead, crease the spine of your new book, get out your cute highlighters, and open up your Bible to the book of Genesis. If you can't find it, here's a hint: It's the first one.

Take some time to read through Genesis 1 - 5. We have a spot for you to take notes if you're feeling extra studious, or if you're more of a skimmer, here are some short summaries of each chapter.

LET'S REVIEW!

01 In the beginning, God created the heavens and the earth. Using His breath of life, God spoke His creation into existence over six days. He proved His creativity and mastery over the earth by creating order out of chaos. Then, after He created man and woman in His image, He blessed them and told them to be fruitful and to rule the earth. On the seventh day He rested.

02 Genesis 2 presents us with another view of Creation: a prelude to the Fall. God breathed life into man and placed him in the beautiful garden of Eden, commanding him to not eat from the tree of the knowledge of good and evil. God saw that it was not good for man to be alone, so He made a companion for him: woman.

03 A serpent (the devil) tempted the man and the woman (Adam and Eve) to doubt God's goodness and authority. They fell for the trick and ate from the tree they were told not to eat from. They tried to hide their sin from God, but He saw their brokenness. God told them the consequences of their actions. These consequences would affect every human being to come after them and would eventually necessitate the rescue mission of Jesus. God removed them from the garden, but only after He took the life of an animal to clothe them and hide their shame. Here we read about the first sacrifice, foreshadowing the ultimate death which took away our shame forever.

04 Adam and Eve gave birth to two sons named Cain and Abel. Cain worked the ground and Abel was a shepherd, so they both presented offerings to God from their respective dominions. God honored Abel's offering over Cain's, and Cain became angry at his brother. Giving in to his sin, Cain murdered his brother and was exiled. God showed mercy on Eve and gave her another son, Seth.

05 Adam and Eve's family line continued to grow and thrive, honoring God's command to be fruitful and multiply (a.k.a. make babies). The descendants are listed in the male line. Enoch, one of these descendants, never died but was instead taken up to be with God. Finally, the genealogy ends with Noah, son of Lamech.

NOTES

_____
_____
_____
_____
_____
_____
_____
_____
_____
_____
_____
_____
_____
_____
_____
_____
_____
_____
_____
_____
_____
_____
_____
_____
_____
_____
_____

 **PRAY THIS PRAYER!**

God, You are so good! There is nothing I would rather be doing right now than learning about Your heart. Please get rid of all the distractions so that I can focus totally on You. Thank You for breathing life into me. I know that in any situation I can seek Your face and find everything I need. Send Your Holy Spirit to guide me as I learn how to choose life over death.

GOD BREATHES LIFE

GENESIS 2:4 - 3:24

As we begin our study of the book of Genesis, we are so excited to focus in on the story that might be one of the most well-known and hotly-contested moments in the Old Testament. This week, we are talking about Creation and the Fall or as we like to call it, "the Fail."[1]

If you ever went to Vacation Bible School or ever sat in a Sunday school class while your parents went to "big church," you're probably familiar with the Creation story. You consider Adam and Eve to be old friends, and you're appropriately embarrassed by their childish behavior that had such huge ramifications. Or if you are new to the church thing, maybe you heard references to Creation in arguments between "faith people" and "science people." What images come to your mind when you think about this story?

+ Doodle your memories of the Adam and Eve story in the space below. What images immediately come to mind?

Did you draw an apple? Maybe a tree? A snake? If you didn't put the sun in the top right-hand corner like we all did as kids, go ahead and fill that in; we won't tell anybody that you forgot. (If you're not a doodler and you skipped this whole part, don't worry. We still love you.)

The first few chapters of Genesis are famous. They're constantly recreated in pop culture (*Twilight* book cover, anybody?), and honestly, the legendary status of the story may have lessened its impact for you when you read your Bible. So let's get back to the basics. Let's read this Scripture with fresh eyes and open hearts, because God has a bigger purpose for this moment in His Word than inspiring the logo most of us have on the back of our cell phones.

Spoiler alert, there's not actually an apple in this story.

Go ahead and read Genesis 2:4 - 7.

Uh oh. We've already run into a problem.

+ For context, copy Genesis 1:1 in the box below.

So . . . God either created the world twice or your Bible has a misprint?

NOPE!

Our Bibles actually have *two accounts of Creation*! The story you have in your mind is probably a hodgepodge of both.

There are a lot of different beliefs about why we get two (slightly different) accounts of Creation. Some people believe that they come from different traditions and were both copy and pasted in to cover all the bases. Some people see the second Creation story as a zoom-in on a single day of the first Creation story. Some people see the first story as general knowledge and the second one as the origin story that is strictly relevant to God's chosen people, the Israelites.

Are you confused yet? Us too. Let's make it simple.

Whatever the reason, God chose for us to have both stories of Creation. So it must be important.

God wants us to hear and learn from His Word even when we don't fully understand. So let's dive in!

> **"This is the account of the heavens and the earth when they were created, when the LORD God made the earth and the heavens."**
> **Genesis 2:4**

Seems like a great place to start! God made the heavens and the earth. That's an important fact. Our God is *Creator*.

Then we see God's creation of the first human paired with a neat little foreshadowing moment to next week in our study when it rains *a lot* (hint: check verse 5).

+ **Fill in the blanks from Genesis 2:7 below.**

"Then the LORD God formed a man from the dust of the ground and breathed into his nostrils the _____ of _____, and the man became a living being."

Here we learn another important fact about God.

Our God *breathes life*.

Highlight verse 7 in your Bible, because we're going to come back to it.

+ Read Genesis 2:8 - 9 and fill in the names of the two trees below.

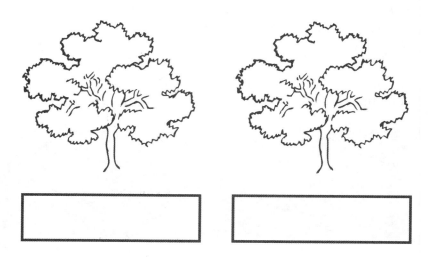

Are you shook yet? There were actually *two* important trees in the middle of the garden in Eden: the tree of life and the tree of the knowledge of good and evil. Imagining the absolute perfection of the garden, we can guess that both of these trees were beautiful, their fruit having the ability to make anyone's mouth water. They were the centerpiece of paradise, the crown jewels of God's home turf. You can bet Adam spent a lot of time lounging in their shade, maybe playing Uno with God or riding a giraffe.

So God placed the human in the garden to work it and take care of it. Then what did He say?

+ Copy Genesis 2:16 - 17 in the box below.

Here the human was given the very first rule: Don't eat from the tree of the knowledge of good and evil. And we learn that it isn't even an arbitrary rule. Eating from the forbidden tree would be *deadly* to the man. So it makes sense that God would have told him to steer clear of it! But pay attention to what God said first.

+ Fill in the blanks from Genesis 2:16b below.

"You are _____ to eat from ____ _____ in the _____;"

Any tree? Really?

+ Think hard, what other tree have we been told about so far in the story?

That's right! *The tree of life!*

The way God issued this command creates a hyperlink in your brain to the two trees the narrator mentioned earlier.

Okay, the human couldn't eat from one tree, but God left the other trees, including the tree of life, wide open and available.

Adam, our human, had the option to *choose life*.

The stakes just got higher. Let's see what happened next.

God realized that the human was lonely so He gave him a helper, the woman. Fun fact: The Hebrew word used for "helper" here is *ezer*. It's a word that is commonly used to describe a desperately needed help that is delivered by the Lord. We love that girl power moment.

They locked eyes, some romantic Taylor Swift song playing in the background, and probably kissed or held hands or something. The Bible's very first marriage. Then the story wraps up with this beautiful line:

> **"Adam and his wife were both naked, and they felt no shame."**
> **Genesis 2:25**

Don't you wish we could just close our books now and be done? That would have been the happiest of endings, but sadly things get *real* shady *real* quickly.

Read Genesis 3:1 - 7.

Wow! A lot just went down. Let's take it piece by piece.

First, Mr. Serpent slithered in and struck up a conversation with the woman.

+ **What is the first question he asks? (3:1)**

Just your average snake, striking up a conversation . . . totally normal . . .

NO!

Don't let the amount of times you've heard this story downplay the weirdness happening here! A snake is talking! That's *freaky*! We're imagining less *Veggie Tales* vibes and more of a creepy doll you found in the attic saying "mama" situation.

This is unnatural. Clearly something else is going on here, something sinister.

This serpent is more than he seems.

Okay, so Satan in snake form rolled up to Eve and questioned God. We can assume our instincts would be telling us to run for the hills, but the woman, fresh to the whole "real world" thing and more innocent than we can imagine, didn't hear any alarm bells going off. She just took the talking snake in stride and answered his question.

> **"The woman said to the serpent, 'We may eat fruit from the trees in the garden, but God did say, "You must not eat fruit from the tree that is in the middle of the garden, and you must not touch it, or you will die."'"**
> **Genesis 3:2 - 3**

Go back and check out God's original command that you copied down (verses 16 - 17). There are some differences, right? Clearly the woman got her information secondhand. Remember, she had not even been made yet when God gave the original command to Adam. Maybe Adam added the "you must not touch it" part for

27

emphasis. But still, she knew the forbidden action and its deadly consequences.

Whereas the serpent was crafty with his first question, slyly questioning God without outright challenging him. His next statement is a punch in the gut. He introduces the straight-up *lie* that what God said would happen, wouldn't actually happen.

+ Fill in the blanks from Genesis 3:5 below.

"For God knows that when you eat from it your _____ _____ be _____, and you will ____ ____ ____, knowing _____ and _____."

Hold up. We need some context.

+ Copy down Genesis 1:27 in the space below.

```


```

The first Creation story gives us an important detail. Humans were made in the *image of God*. So it's almost ridiculous that Satan is tempting the woman with the idea of "being like God."

They were made to be like God!

Created in His mighty image, these two humans were made with the full potential to be like God. Heck, God already gave them important, God-like duties (see Genesis 2:19)!

He taught them, spent time with them, and slowly matured them, all under the shade of the tree of life.

So being "like God" was already on the table! The decision the snake offered was something else.

Would they take God at His word and do it His way, or would they take matters into their own hands?

+ **Think of a time in your life when you were faced with a decision and you chose wrong. What were the ramifications?**

```
┌─────────────────────────────────────────────┐
│                                             │
│                                             │
│                                             │
│                                             │
│                                             │
│                                             │
│                                             │
└─────────────────────────────────────────────┘
```

We all know the end of this story. The woman chose death, thinking it was life, and her husband did the same. And just like that, their eyes were opened. But instead of opening their eyes to a new, more God-like world, what did they see?

"Then the eyes of both of them were opened, and they realized that they were naked; so they sewed fig leaves together and made coverings for themselves."
Genesis 3:7

They failed. They chose the "do it yourself" path, rejecting God's plan, and right when they were supposed to suddenly become superheroes, they looked down and found themselves naked.

This moment is *so* significant, and it's a moment we can all relate to.

The moment that Adam and his wife chose death, they realized that they were unprepared, uncovered, and insignificant. They looked down at their newly "independent" selves and saw only lack.

How can we be like God when we don't even have clothes?

Have you ever been there? You try so hard to do everything on your own, ignoring God's good plan, because you think your way is better. And suddenly you get exactly where you wanted to be, but you realize that you're naked.

You're alone. You're unequipped.

You realize the loving Father you ditched to race ahead is actually the one holding the key.

You were wrong, and now you're stripped.

This *Fall* really is more like a *Fail*. Our ancient ancestors had everything at their fingertips. The tree of life was literally two steps away! But they threw it all away, forfeiting the life that God offered.

So what did God do?

Read Genesis 3:8 - 13.

This passage paints a portrait of a gentle God. He asked questions to which He already knew the answers in order to give His beloved children the chance to respond. You can almost hear the tenderness in His voice, the heartbreak.

"What is this you have done?"
Genesis 3:13b

The humans, brand new to shame and sin, didn't know how to respond to His tender questions. They were quick to use their new instincts of blame and denial. The man blamed his wife and the woman blamed the snake, but nobody asked for forgiveness or direction from the clearly open-hearted Father who stood before them.

We can almost imagine God taking a deep breath, ready to inform His kids of the consequences that their actions had already set in motion.

Read Genesis 3:14 - 19.

+ Who or what was cursed?

Right. The serpent now has to slither, and the ground will not bear fruit with its former ease.

Notice how God didn't curse the humans. Sure, their actions would have big consequences that would affect their lives greatly, but God wasn't in the business of dooming them without hope.

+ Go back to Genesis 2:7. What attribute of God did we learn here?

Our God is a *life-breather*. Even more specifically, He gave His miraculous breath of life to the humans, His children. Do you really think He would curse them so quickly? After one, admittedly giant, mistake?

That's not the character of our God.

In fact even in His lamenting, when He delivered punishment and consequence, He couldn't help but to offer hope.

Okay, so maybe you aren't immediately seeing the hope in this verse. This, right here, is actually the first declaration of the Gospel!

> **"And I will put enmity between you and the woman, and between your offspring and hers; he will crush your head, and you will strike his heel."**
> **Genesis 3:15**

God prophesied that a descendant of the woman, our Savior Jesus, would be the one to crush the head of the snake. Jesus would be the one to finally win the victory over the devil!

"It was as if God could not wait to announce His plan of salvation, to bring deliverance through the one known as the Seed of the woman."[2]

Whoa. Read that again.

Here in the very beginning of the Bible, God already laid out His rescue plan. We're only a couple verses out from the Big Fail and God stepped in with His mission to bring His children back to Him.

Why? Because our God can't help but *breathe life*.

GOSPEL LENS

Jesus Christ, the Son of God and offspring of the woman, was sent for our redemption. He came to earth and lived the perfect life that we, just like Adam and Eve, could never live. He died, taking our burdens upon himself and rose again three days later, claiming victory over the devil and offering us eternal life in Eden paradise with Him. WOW! That's good news!

HARD TRUTH TIME!

+ What is one area in your life that you need God to breathe new life into? Why?

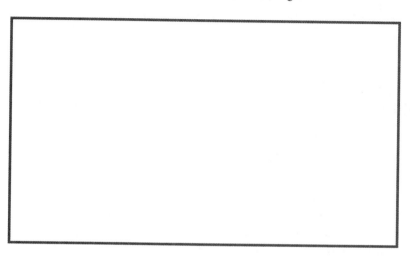

+ Be honest, how much hope do you have in God's ability to breathe new life into your situation?

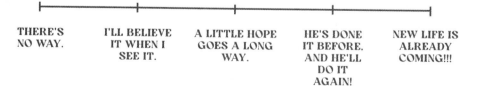

THERE'S NO WAY.	I'LL BELIEVE IT WHEN I SEE IT.	A LITTLE HOPE GOES A LONG WAY.	HE'S DONE IT BEFORE, AND HE'LL DO IT AGAIN!	NEW LIFE IS ALREADY COMING!!!

Adam recognized it, too. He heard the hope that God offered. In fact, we see him name his wife Eve (verse 20), the mother of all the living. He knew that, from her offspring, the tree of life would become available to God's children again.

Read Genesis 3:21 - 24.

Our God wasn't kidding when He kicked 'em out of Eden. (If you're into '90s worship music you'll get that reference. If not, we can make you a killer Spotify playlist.) God knew his newly sin-driven kids couldn't take from the tree of life now; it was too dangerous. He knew Adam and Eve couldn't live like Hannah Montana, having one foot in both worlds. So they had to leave.

But what did He do first? *He clothed them.*

God saw Adam and Eve's attempt to cover their inadequacies and took pity on them. He killed an animal, one of His precious creations, and made them new clothes from its skin.

We are so quick to judge Adam and Eve. We think they made a dumb mistake, and we blame them for the state of the world we have to live in. But really we are *all* Adam and Eve. We stare right at the tree of life as we take the forbidden fruit of self-sufficiency. We walk boldly into the path of death only to find ourselves naked, bloody, bruised, and in desperate need of a Savior.

Thankfully, we have a God who sends His Spirit to breathe new life into us. Are you ready to take a deep breath of God's grace? Can you taste His hope on your tongue?

Maybe your forbidden fruit is that guy you've been seeing that you know isn't good for you.

Maybe you're a people pleaser, always trying to be perfect and hating yourself when you miss the mark.

Maybe you keep running back to porn, sex, alcohol, or drugs, because it's "no big deal."

Maybe you have never tasted God's spirit and never accepted Jesus's offer of life.

Whatever your pain point is, the character of our God doesn't change. He *is* a life-breather and He *will* breathe new life into your situation, no matter how desperate and desolate it may seem.

Here and now, we all get the opportunity to accept God's gift of life. We get to stop choosing death. Reach out your hand, and allow your tender and loving God to clothe you in new righteousness. His plan was always to rescue you. It's time to believe it.

THINK IT THROUGH . . .

WHAT STOOD OUT TO YOU?

WHAT CONVICTED YOU?

WHAT DO YOU FEEL CALLED TO SHARE?

CONVERSATION STARTERS

+ What is an area of your life that you are currently choosing your way over God's way?

_____

_____

_____

_____

+ What is holding you back from fully embracing God's design for your life? How might it be affecting your relationship with Him?

_____

_____

_____

_____

_____

_____

_____

+ Think of that area of your life where you need God's breath of life. What would it look like for you to choose His way today?

_____

_____

_____

_____

_____

_____

_____

_____

_____

CHAPTER 2

GOD IS GOOD WHEN
THINGS ARE BAD

GENESIS
CHAPTERS 6-10

Now that we've all cried ourselves out from that WORD from the Lord last week, we are feeling fresh and ready to jump into week two of Genesis! Genesis is full of hard, controversial, and wrestle-worthy topics, so get ready because this second week is about to be a bit of a workout.

It's always good to stretch before you do theological pilates, right? Go ahead and read through Genesis 6 - 10. Just like last week, we have space for you to take notes as you read or summaries if you're running low on time.

LET'S REVIEW!

06 Mankind multiplied and grew more and more evil, consumed with their sin. God decided to give them over to their sin, allowing a great flood to wipe out the earth and everything on it. But He chose Noah and his family to carry on the human race. He instructed Noah to build an ark and to fill it with two of every creature.

07 Noah, his family, and two of every creature with the breath of life in them entered the ark just like God said. The Flood came, and it rained for forty days and forty nights. Everything outside of the ark was wiped out, until only those in the ark were left.

08 Eventually the waters receded and God told Noah and his family it was okay to come out. Noah immediately built an altar to the Lord and offered sacrifices to Him. God was pleased by the offering and promised never to destroy all living creatures with a flood again.

09 God established His covenant with Noah, telling him to be fruitful and multiply and giving him some guidelines to live by. Next God made the promise again to never send a flood to destroy the earth. He chose a rainbow to be a reminder of this promise. Then Noah became drunk and stirred up some family drama, causing one of his sons to be cursed. Finally at 950 years old, he died.

10 This chapter lays out the ancestral line of Noah and his sons. These descendants spread out into the land, obeying God's command for multiplication.

NOTES

_____
_____
_____
_____
_____
_____
_____
_____
_____
_____
_____
_____
_____
_____
_____
_____
_____
_____
_____
_____
_____
_____
_____
_____

 **PRAY THIS PRAYER!**

God, You are totally and completely good, all of the time! You are always praiseworthy, even in the worst of times. I'm sorry for when my current situation has clouded my vision, and I'm sorry for when I let my circumstances influence my thoughts about You. Thank You for Your endless grace and Your commitment to rescue and mercy. Please help me to see You more clearly as I learn to hold tight to who You say You are.

GOD IS GOOD WHEN THINGS ARE BAD

GENESIS 6:5 - 9:17

Do you remember the day Snapchat introduced filters? You would have thought the world exploded. Suddenly everyone was taking selfies with the cute little dog ears and sticking their tongue out to trigger the animation. We thought it was *so* cool, especially because we had never seen anything like it before.

Nowadays, you can't run across an Instagram pic or a TikTok video that doesn't have some sort of filter on it. You know that one that makes you look like a supermodel? Yup, definitely damaging for your self-image but great when you don't want to put makeup on to film your OOTD.

This week of our study, as we explore the story of Noah and the Flood, we learn how to read the Bible *unfiltered*. When you want to encounter the truth of who God is, you need to cut out all the extra things your sinful nature wants to add to the image. It's no vintage grain, no beauty filter, no puppy dog ears . . . it's just TRUTH. And that raw, unfiltered truth of God is what has the power to truly set you free.

We need to take off all the filters and see God for who He is.

Are you ready? Let's dive in!

Read Genesis 6:5 - 7.

Hardcore, right? We went from God creating woodland creatures and talking snakes last week to "I'm going to destroy the world."

Yikes.

What does the Bible say caused this 180 degree turn?

+ Fill in the blanks from Genesis 6:5.

"The LORD saw how great the wickedness of the human race had become on the earth, and that _____ _____ of the thoughts of the _____ _____ was _____ _____ all the time."

In our world of exaggeration and reality TV, it might be easy to assume that this is overstated. But this is *God* observing the world. His observations are always spot-on! So when He said that *every* inclination of the human heart was *always* evil, that's exactly what He meant.

The whole world was corrupted only six chapters after it was made.

If you've been reading along with us, this is no surprise to you! We've seen fratricide (Cain killing Abel in Genesis 3:5), polygamy (Lamech in Genesis 3:19), more murder (Lamech again in Genesis 3:23), and even angel rebellion (Genesis 6:1). The world was on a lightspeed journey to total ruin, and God couldn't just stand by and watch His beloved creation continue to fall.

We read in verse 6 that God was "deeply troubled." This is important to know, especially as we are acclimating to our new "unfiltered" reading.

+ Find John 3:16 and copy it in the space below.

What do we know about God? What caused him to be "deeply troubled" at the state of His creation?

+ Fill in the blank.

God _____ the world.

That's right! God LOVES His creation! Keep that in mind as we continue this story. Allow it to affect the way you read what happens next.

God declared that He would wipe out the whole human race and all of the creatures on the ground and in the sky, mourning the fact that He had ever made them. But then, there's a twist.

> ## "But Noah found favor in the eyes of the LORD."
> **Genesis 6:8**

This is the turning point, the light in an otherwise dark situation. Grace found Noah.[1]

If we believe what God said, that everything was evil and doomed, we have to assume that Noah couldn't have earned God's grace. In fact, that's not even how grace works! Grace has to be *unearned*! That's what makes it such a miraculous gift.

We can picture a heartbroken God surveying the world He made, His eyes finally resting on one man. His heart softens, and He changes His mind.

We can almost hear His thought process . . .

You know what? I won't wipe out the whole human race. I will save them! I will choose Noah as the carrier of My hope.

Ahh. We're starting to see His love.

Let's continue on. Read Genesis 6:9 - 22.

Verse 9 never fails to make us laugh. We learn that, in fact, Noah was:

". . . blameless among the people of his time . . ."

What an accomplishment! That's like getting a 50% on the test that the rest of your class got 30% on. There's something to be said for a low bar.

But before you go on hating on our boy Noah, check out how he responded to God when He laid out His plan.

God told Noah that He was going to put an end to all people, so Noah needed to build a really big boat and get in there with his family and two of every kind of animal. And what did Noah do?

+ Copy down Genesis 6:22 in the box below.

Okay, so maybe Noah was a little bit cooler than we thought. This dude had never even seen rain (remember our foreshadowing moment from last week?) and probably didn't have a master's degree in zoology, but he obeyed *completely*.

Check out Hebrews 11:7:

> "By faith Noah, when warned about things not yet seen, in holy fear built an ark to save his family. By his faith he condemned the world and became heir of the righteousness that is in keeping with faith."
> Hebrews 11:7

It seems like Noah had his perspective set. Despite the world he lived in, Noah must have known the character of his God. He had faith in His goodness, even when God told him about the devastation that was to come.

What can we learn from Noah?

We need to read stories like this through the lens of what we know about God. God is good, and everything He does is good. How is this story an act of His goodness?

+ Have you ever wondered why God allows bad things to happen? What brought you to this question?

Okay, now we've hit the action. Chapter 7 starts with God giving Noah the go-ahead to move into the ark. Stuff is about to go down. Again, we see Noah's trust in God.

> ## "And Noah did all that the LORD commanded him."
> **Genesis 7:5**

Noah and his fam obediently loaded up on the ark with about a zillion animals, and the flood waters came. This is an apocalyptic moment. The New Interpreter's Study Bible describes it like this:

"Israel's God, who brought order from chaos, now allows chaos to return."[2]

God was undoing all of the good work He had done. And knowing what we know about God's character, we know that He was not enjoying Himself. As He allowed the world to go where it was trying to go (total destruction) He was mourning the tragic loss of all of the people He had shared His own breath with.

+ Copy down Genesis 7:22 in the space below.

Go back to what you wrote and circle "breath of life."

Does that sound familiar? Flip back to week 1 if you need a refresher.

The Hebrew word here that distinguishes this as the breath of life is *ruah*.

We saw *ruah* pop up in Genesis 6:17 and 7:15, and we'll see it again.

+ **Fill in the blank from Genesis 8:1.**

"But God remembered Noah and all the wild animals and the livestock that were with him in the ark, and he sent a _____ over the earth, and the waters receded."

Guess what word translates as "wind"?

Ruah.

SYMBOLISM ALERT!

God sent His *ruah* to calm the waters. His spirit, His breath, was the clear marker of hope in this story.

God was true to His character. He was always going to breathe life.

God *will* always breathe life.

Maybe you are getting to this point and your stomach is starting to squirm a little. Your body is uncomfortable, because your eyes can't help but see a contradiction.

God just literally destroyed the world! How can He still be a life-breather?

This is where all the filters need to come off so we can start fresh.

What do we know about God so far?

1. God breathes life.
2. God loves the world.
3. God is good (read 1 Chronicles 16:34 for proof).

There's this parable in the New Testament where Jesus talks about people building houses on different kinds of foundations. In the story Jesus compares someone who hears God's truth—specifically the truth He presents in His famous "Sermon on the Mount"—but disregards it, to a person who builds a house on the sand. The second a storm comes, the whole house comes crashing down. But what about the person who allows God's truth to really sink into her heart and mind?

"Therefore everyone who hears these words of mine and puts them into practice is like a wise man who built his house on the rock. The rain came down, the streams rose, and the winds blew and beat against that house; yet it did not fall, because it had its foundation on the rock."
Matthew 7:24 - 25

It seems like the Bible is telling us that our *foundation* is important when we encounter storms.

So how can we apply this to Noah's storm?

At first glance, God's judgement here seems harsh and scary. How could He allow everything on the earth to die? Even further, how can Christians be okay with serving a God who does things like that?

Maybe this seems too far off, too much like a fairy tale for you to really understand the horror. But apply it to your own storm.

How could God allow my mom to get cancer? She's done nothing but love Him and serve Him her whole life!

How could God let a pandemic rage across the world? Is He even paying attention?

How could God be okay with all of the hurt and trauma I had to go through? Does He even care at all?

Do you feel it? That sinking feeling in your stomach, that tug on your heart toward despair?

Noah must have felt that, too. He must have had some friends out there in the world, no matter how much he disagreed with their lifestyles. He must have mourned the loss of everything he had known. He must have had moments where it all seemed like too much. But still, he did everything the Lord commanded him.

How?

Noah built his foundation on the rock.

Look back at the story of the Flood, but this time, start with what you know to be true about God instead of what your clouded eyes see about the situation Noah was faced with.

God is good. And that good God sent a flood to destroy the world.

God loves the world. And that loving God wiped out everything He had carefully and intentionally created.

God breathes life. And that life-breathing God withdrew His breath of life from His creation.

Lean into the contradictions!!

HARD TRUTH TIME!

+ Think of an area or situation in your life that is difficult to look at through a God-lens. Use the space below to write out all of your honest and unfiltered thoughts. Why is it so hard to trust Him in this area?

+ **What aspect of God's character do you want to focus on as you wrestle through your storm (e.g., His goodness, His kindness, His love, etc.)?**

You're right. It doesn't make sense that a good God would allow bad things to happen. But we trust that God is good. So we know that if He is allowing a bad thing to happen, it *must* ultimately be for good.

It seems crazy that a God who loves the world would allow it to be devastated. But we trust God's love for His children and stand on a firm, rock foundation. So the Flood must have been an act of His love.

How could a God who breathes life turn around and take that life away?

It must be with the purpose to bring new life again.

Noah's foundation helped him see the hope that God was offering. Let's find that hope for ourselves!

Read Genesis 8:18 - 22.

After a whole year in the ark, God told Noah and his family it was finally safe to come out. The waters receded and dry land was available again. It must have been a crazy moment. I bet everyone kissed the ground, high fived each other, and relished the feeling of grass between their toes.

What did Noah do?

+ Check Genesis 8:20 to see what Noah did when he exited the ark and write it in the space below.

[   ]

You got it! He built an altar to the Lord! Man, if this isn't proof of his firm foundation in God's goodness, we don't know what is! He had just spent a year floating around in a giant wooden box while the world fell apart around him and the first thing he did when he was finally freed was praise the Lord.

Noah understood the character of His God and decided He was worthy of praise, even in desolation.

We read that God smelled Noah's sacrificial offering and it pleased Him.

Noah's sacrifice, his total faith in God's character, and his submission to God's will unlocked the hope that the world needed and the hope that God was itching to provide. God says that He will never again destroy all living creatures with a flood, *even though mankind was still inclined to evil.*

GOSPEL LENS

Sacrifice is pleasing to God! For years, God's people had to atone for their sins through ritual sacrifices, paying the blood price that was due for all of their brokenness. But God knew all along that He would send His son Jesus to be the final and complete atoning sacrifice for our sins. Jesus's total obedience to His Father paid the price we couldn't pay and allowed us to approach God as blameless and forgiven children forever.

"God's grace operates not despite human sin but because of human sin."[3]

God's plan is coming a little more into focus. He started fresh with Noah, marking His promise on his sacrifice; His full attention on the rescue He knew was coming.

Remember last week when we heard God promise the Messiah? He had not forgotten! Noah's sacrifice and his faith were another building block to the great plan of Jesus. His children needed a final rescue. They needed Jesus.

Read Genesis 9:8 - 17.

Woo! As we are closing out this crazy story, we are introduced to an important concept that you will need to keep in your back pocket for later.

Covenant.

We will see more covenants pop up later as we continue on in our Genesis adventure, but this one is special because it's the only covenant that is one-sided and unconditional. God promised to never destroy the earth again and asked for nothing in return from Noah or his family. This was a pure, genuine promise from God. We know that He will always keep it.

God, always looking to add beauty, then set a rainbow in the sky as a reminder of this promise. Noah and his family could always look up when it rained and find comfort in the rainbow. It was a reminder of God's trustworthiness and His goodness.

The rainbow continues to remind us that our God loves the world.

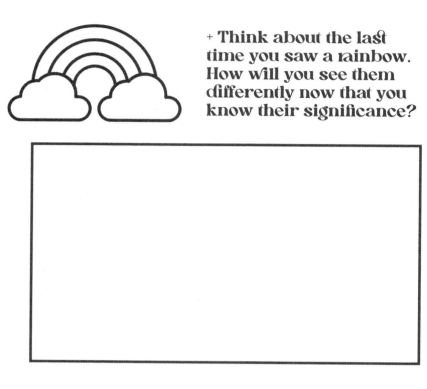

+ **Think about the last time you saw a rainbow. How will you see them differently now that you know their significance?**

+ **Okay, to wrap this all up, find 2 Peter 3:9 and fill in the blanks below.**

"The Lord is not _____ in keeping his _____, as some understand slowness. Instead he is _____ with you, not wanting anyone to _____, but everyone to come to _____ ."

God did not sit back and enjoy the Flood. It didn't please Him to watch His creation die. His heart was most certainly in mourning.

So why didn't He step in? Why didn't He stop it and save everyone?

Our good, loving, and patient Father knew that the Flood was the only way for His promise of salvation to be fulfilled. His judgement of the world here was a *mercy*. It was an opportunity for the repentance and ultimate salvation of His children to come.

What does that mean for us? How can we trust in God's goodness when the world seems anything but good, when it seems only evil all the time?

We stand firm on who we know our God to be.

It's okay if you are still torn. It's okay if you aren't able to look at your situation and see God's goodness in it. The question of why bad things happen has plagued humanity for ages, and it's not a question we can answer firmly or give a quick fix to.

But we can look for hope like Noah did.

Think back on your storm, whatever it is, and try to see it through your God-filter. See how He mourns with you at the pain and brokenness all around, but also see that His goodness *must* overcome and that His love *will* make a way.

That's just who He is.

THINK IT THROUGH . . .

WHAT STOOD OUT TO YOU?

WHAT CONVICTED YOU?

WHAT DO YOU FEEL CALLED TO SHARE?

CONVERSATION STARTERS

+ What storm have you encountered or are currently facing that has made it hard to trust God's goodness?

_____

_____

_____

_____

+ Think about your foundation. What aspect of God's character might you be seeing incorrectly? Why?

_____

_____

_____

_____

_____

_____

_____

+ Apply God's goodness and love to your storm. What starts to look different about it now?

_____

_____

_____

_____

_____

_____

_____

_____

_____

CHAPTER 3

GOD KEEPS YOU SAFE
BUT CALLS YOU TO SCARY

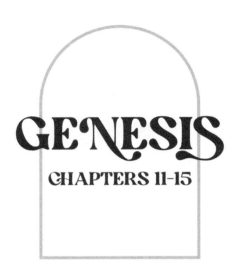

GENESIS
CHAPTERS 11-15

You look like you need to take a few deep breaths. It's necessary after that *heavy* topic last week. Go ahead. We'll wait!

Do you feel better now? Great! Let's jump into week 3 of Genesis! This week we hit one of the lesser known stories of Genesis, but it's one of the most important. The story of Abraham literally sets the tone and vision for the *rest of the Bible*. Get excited! Read through Genesis 11 - 15 or take a glance at these summaries to help you prepare for this week's lesson.

LET'S REVIEW!

11 This chapter begins with the story behind how and why different nations have different languages. Some people decided to build a tower of Babylon that would stretch to the heavens so that they could make a name for themselves. They wanted to elevate themselves over God. So God, knowing the danger in this line of thinking, scattered them and scrambled their vocabulary, creating different languages and cultures.

12 God called a man named Abram, a descendant of Noah, to leave his homeland and go to a place that God would show him. He promised to bless Abram and to make him a great nation through which the whole world would be blessed. Abram set out with his wife Sarai and his nephew Lot to see the land that God had promised them. When a famine hit, they traveled to Egypt where Abram lied to Pharaoh about his relationship with Sarai out of fear. Luckily, the Lord intervened and saved them from that sticky situation.

13 As Abram and his family kept traveling, their combined property grew too large to stay together. Abram suggested that he and Lot part ways amicably. Lot chose to go one way, so Abram went the other.

14 Four kings banded together to take over the region near where Abram and his family were living. When Abram learned that they had captured Lot and his family, he came to the rescue and defeated the enemy. After Abram saved Lot, a king and high priest named Melchizedek blessed him and acknowledged God's hand in his life.

15 God reminded Abram of His promise to him when Abram was beginning to doubt His plan. God told Abram that his descendants would be as numerous as the stars, even though Abram and Sarai were unable to have kids.

NOTES

_____
_____
_____
_____
_____
_____
_____
_____
_____
_____
_____
_____
_____
_____
_____
_____
_____
_____
_____
_____
_____
_____
_____
_____

PRAY THIS PRAYER!

God, You are so big, so mighty, and so in control. Yet somehow You
are still tender, intimate, and full of empathy. I'm sorry for when
I let my fear make my decisions for me. Please cleanse me of all my
distractions so that I can focus fully on You. Thank You for endless
new grace and Your perfect understanding. Guide me as I follow
Your call into the unknown. You have my trust.

GOD KEEPS YOU SAFE BUT CALLS YOU TO SCARY

GENESIS 12:1 - 9, 15:1 - 21

Google is your best friend and your worst enemy when it comes to studying the Bible. We all find ourselves searching up Bible verses or random questions, then taking whatever first three options pop up as the truth. So let's all say it together:

Google is a great tool, but Google is not God.

Don't worry, we're all guilty, but we're sure that God has an extra reserve of "Google grace" in heaven somewhere.

Right now though, we want you to Google this:

Does God keep us safe?

+ Take some quick notes on what you find in your Google search.

According to Google, the answer is, in fact, yes. God *does* keep us safe. If you were extra thorough with your research, maybe you were led to Psalm 91. That is a great place to start, so let's read it together!

Read Psalm 91.

> **"Whoever dwells in the shelter of the Most High will rest in the shadow of the Almighty. I will say of the LORD, 'He is my refuge and my fortress, my God, in whom I trust.'"**
> **Psalm 91:1 - 2**

This Psalm is straight up *beautiful*. We can appreciate the well-crafted poetry and the topic that hits home. This is the Psalm you send to your friend when she's hiding in the bathtub during a tornado warning or if she just got in a car accident. The image of our Father as a protective fortress is exactly what we need in scary moments.

+ Go through Psalm 91 in your Bible, and circle every time it says "easy."

How many times did you circle? Hint: It should be zero.

+ This time circle every time something scary is mentioned in Psalm 91.

The truth of this Psalm is a necessary foundation for what we are reading today. Are you seeing the message?

+ Rewrite this week's title in the space below.

Yes, our God certainly is our protector and strong fortress, but that doesn't mean we will never encounter trials.

The parking brake is off, so let's roll.

Read Genesis 12:1 - 3.

You just read one of the thesis statements of the Bible. Crazy, right? It may not seem important now, but God's words to Abram here are foundational. We'll go into more detail later, but imagine this as the moment when Elle Woods decides that she is going to go to Harvard Law School. The whole story is set up right here, the plot is about to unravel, and you, as the reader, should be on the edge of your seat.

+ Just so you don't forget, rewrite Genesis 12:2 - 3 in the space below.

Before we get any further, let's stop and read our new friend Abram's Facebook bio. (We say Facebook instead of Instagram because Abram is seventy-five years old at this point in Scripture, and we all know that old people *love* Facebook). Luckily, there are no friend requests needed to track down who Abram is related to.

+ Find Genesis 9:18. Who is the first son mentioned?

```

```

+ Now flip to Genesis 11:10 and skim through Shem's family line. Stop when you get to Terah in verse 26. Who was Terah's first son?

```

```

Woo! We made it through some weird names and tedious reading. So Noah had a son named Shem who was the great-great-great-(and more greats)-grandfather of our friend Abram. And, as if to make matters more confusing, God gave Abram a new name in Genesis 17, Abraham, which is how the New Testament refers to him. But we'll get to that in week 4. Let's keep moving forward.

+ Read Matthew 1:1 – 2. Who is listed here as a descendant of Abraham?

```

```

Yup. That's right. Jesus Christ, the Messiah, Savior of the world.

Abram has an impressive lineage. The author clearly wants you to connect his ancestry with God's rescue plan that we've talked about over the last two weeks. Abram, descendant of Noah, is an ancestor of Jesus.

Whoops! We're having a *That's So Raven* moment and getting way too far ahead of ourselves. Right now, at the beginning of his story, Abram is *not* impressive. Everyone was a descendant of Noah, remember? So Abram was just a regular guy, an ordinary nobody.

But just like Noah, grace found Abram.

Genesis 11 also tells us that Abram had a wife named Sarai who was not able to conceive, so they had no children. That's a big bummer for Abram and makes God's promise of becoming a great nation even more unlikely. Then we learn that Abram settled in Harran, right outside of Canaan, after his father Terah died.

Beware, you're going to be hit with a lot of ancient near-east location names this week. Here's a map to help you visualize.[1]

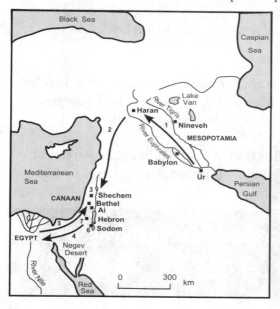

So now that we have some background, let's take another look at what God said to Abram.

> "Go from your country, your people and your father's household to the land I will show you."
> **Genesis 12:1**

We are already reminded of Psalm 91. God, who is Abram's fortress and place of safety, asked him to leave everything behind and go out into a scary world. But to cushion the blow, God gave Abram a covenant. God said He will make Abram into a great nation and through him, all the people of the world will be blessed. But why is this so special?

"A covenant is a chosen relationship or partnership in which two parties make binding promises to each other and work together to reach a common goal."[2]

So we already know that God chose Abram, just like He chose Noah, because He wanted to use Abram in His big plan.
But . . . what's the big plan? What's the "common goal" that these two partners are working toward? Why does Abram need to go to Canaan? Why is it so important that his own kids become a great nation?

The best way to explain the significance of God's promise to Abram in Genesis 12 is to spoil the ending for you. And it's okay! The author of Genesis was writing it years after a lot of the story had unfolded. They knew where the story was headed, so we should, too!

The "great nation" that God promised to Abram was the Israelites. They are the main characters of the rest of the Old Testament. We follow their story as God used them to achieve His big plan.

And that "big plan" that God was hatching is a common thread throughout the whole Bible. He hinted at it right there in the covenant with Abram.

> **"... and all peoples on earth will be blessed through you."**
> **Genesis 12:3b**

God was determined to bring His children back to Him. He wanted every one of His human creations to be blessed. He hadn't given up the rescue that He introduced in Eden and carried on with Noah. Abram was the next in line to join the mission, and *the mission was Jesus.*

And what's this land God is leading Abram to? It's Canaan or "the Promised Land" as it will be referred to throughout the Old Testament. It's a fertile and beautiful piece of land that stretches between the Euphrates and the Nile (check your map for reference) that will later become the kingdom of Israel. Are you ready to be hit in the head with the symbolism hammer again? This Promised Land is referred to as "paradise." The new Eden.

We can think of an obvious moment when all the people on earth were blessed. In fact, they actually received the *ultimate blessing*! When Jesus—a descendant of God's chosen Abram—willingly went to the cross, He was the fulfillment of God's rescue mission. God had you in His mind all the way back in Genesis. He always wanted to save you.

That all sounds like a pretty good deal, especially for a guy who can't have kids. God's promise must have seemed worth the risk though, because we read that Abram set out just as God commanded. Well . . . almost.

+ Fill in the blanks from Genesis 12:4a.

"So Abram went, as the LORD had told him; and _____ _____ _____ _____."

That's what God gets for choosing an average Joe for His big plan. The guy didn't even know how to follow directions right! God specifically told Abram to leave his people and his fathers house, but Abram still brought his nephew Lot along. Spoiler alert: Lot caused Abram *a lot* of trouble. (Sorry for the pun, but we couldn't resist.)

Nevertheless, they went on their way to Canaan and started a cute little road trip tour of the land that God had promised them.

Now let's flip to Genesis 15. Here's what you missed in the between chapters (you can also check out the summaries at the beginning of this chapter):

+ Abram quickly left the Promised Land because of a famine and went to Egypt.

+ Abram lied that his hot wife Sarai was his sister, and God had to rescue her from Pharaoh's harem.

+ After finally returning from Egypt, Lot and Abram split amicably.

+ Lot got into trouble, and Abram had to go save him.

+ A random priest of Abram's God blessed him and reaffirmed God's plan for his life.

If you're craving a crazy, theological rabbit hole, do some research on Melchizedek. You'll thank us later.

Read Genesis 15:1 - 7.

This chapter, much like chapter 12, starts off with a Word from the Lord.

+ Fill in the blanks from Genesis 15:1.

"Do not be _____, Abram. I am your _____, your very great _____."

When you read the Bible often, you pick up on little patterns that happen throughout. We have just encountered one. Usually, when

God told someone not to be afraid, it meant they were *freaking the heck out*.

Right here in Genesis 15, it's pretty clear that Abram must have been in panic mode. He had given up his whole life (or most of it) to follow God into unknown territory. He had been doing an RV tour across Canaan and crazy things kept going down. It was enough to fray anyone's nerves. But in verses 2 and 3, Abram reveals the fear that was really weighing on his heart.

+ What was Abram's main concern in Genesis 15:2 - 3?

Abram thought there was a flaw in God's plan. God had promised to make Abram a great nation but here he was, still childless and getting older by the day. His bold honesty here is a great example of how to pray.[3] God knows that following Him can be scary. He definitely isn't surprised that you can't see where He is leading you.

It's okay to ask for clarity.

The way God answered Abram's desperate prayer reveals a lot about His character.

> "He took him outside and said, 'Look up at the sky and count the stars—if indeed you can count them.' Then he said to him, 'So shall your offspring be.'"
> Genesis 15:5

Choosing faith in God is a risk, especially from an earthly perspective, and God knows that. He is not unsympathetic to your questions and your doubts! We see that so clearly in His tender answer to Abram. He didn't reprimand Abram for asking for clarity. Instead, He reminded Abram of His promise, while also reminding Abram of His plan.

God knew that Abram's courage was directly tied to his vision.

God's answer to Abram was crazy in its depth and layers. Let's dig in!

+ What moment from last week does this remind you of? Hint: God used something in the sky to remind someone of His promise.

```
[                                                    ]
```

You got it! The rainbow. As the rainbow was a symbol of God's faithfulness, so the stars are now a symbol of the same. God had made a promise to Abram that He would give him children and make him a great nation. Every time Abram looked at the night sky, he could be reminded of that covenant. But this is also a reminder of *another* promise.

+ Find Revelation 22:16 and copy it down in the space below.

```
[                                                    ]
```

Jesus is the bright Morning Star. MIND BLOWN! God was not only reminding Abram of His promise to provide him a biological child, but He was also foreshadowing Abram's many-greats-

03 / GENESIS 11-15

grandson who would be the Savior of the world, the seed who would fulfill the chasm that was created in the garden.

+ **Think of a time when you doubted God's plan for your life. Did you go to God with your worries like Abram did? Why or why not?**

Okay, now we are hitting the climax of our story this week. Elle Woods has finally realized that she doesn't need Warner after all and that being a lawyer-fashion-icon is actually her passion. We're in the courtroom. Let's see what happens next.

+ **Fill in the blanks from Genesis 15:6.**

"Abram _____ the _____ , and he _____ it to him as _____ ."

This verse, when read with the right context, is one of the clearest beacons of hope in the Old Testament. It's the key to understanding what Jesus did for you. It's the introduction of the free gift of *grace*.

+ **Check out Galatians 3:5 - 9.**

"So again I ask, does God give you his Spirit and work miracles among you by the works of the law, or by your believing what you heard? So also Abraham 'believed God, and it was credited to him as righteousness.' Understand, then, that those who have faith are children of Abraham. Scripture foresaw that God would justify the Gentiles by faith, and announced the gospel in advance to Abraham: 'All nations will be blessed through you.' So those who rely on faith are blessed along with Abraham, the man of faith."
Galatians 3:5 - 9

+ **Take some time and summarize these verses in your own words. What does it mean for your life?**

Grace found Abram. It was not his actions, his obedience, or his success that made him righteous in the eyes of God. All he did was believe what God said to him.

And you know what? Grace found *you*.

Grace found you before you had done anything to earn it. You could *never* earn it! Grace found you when you were right in the middle of your darkest moments. It found you when you were desperate, empty, and in need of saving.

> **"for,** "EVERYONE WHO CALLS ON THE NAME OF THE LORD WILL BE SAVED."
> **Romans 10:13**

Abram was saved. His faith brought him into the protection of a good God. He was counted as righteous in the presence of a perfect King, just like us when we call on the name of the Lord and choose faith in Him for eternal life.

Abram was safe, eternally speaking, but he was still an alien in a foreign land. He was still childless and old. He was still scared.

So what do we know about God?

God calls us to risky steps of faith.

HARD TRUTH TIME!

+ **If God asked you to step out in faith right now, whatever that might look like for you, how willing would you be to obey?**

HE'S NEVER ASKED ME TO DO ANYTHING! — DEFINITELY NOT. — MAYBE IF HE DRAGGED ME INTO IT. — PROBABLY, AS LONG AS IT ISN'T TOO SCARY . . . — HECK YES! ANYTHING! SIGN ME UP!

+ **Was there ever a moment in your life when you placed your full trust in Jesus? If yes, what was it like? If not, what has been holding you back?**

Abram trusted in God's promise and followed up that trust with obedience. But we see that his life with God was not smooth sailing. It wasn't pretty, and it wasn't easy. In fact, in the next few verses, God told Abram about the trials he was going to have to endure.

Read Genesis 15:13.

Abram's descendants would be enslaved! His own flesh and blood would be mistreated, while under the protection of their Lord. And looking even further ahead, the Israelites would not even claim the Promised Land until *700 years later*! We will find as we read Genesis, that the rest of Abram's story was often brutal and difficult.

Yet Abram walked with the Lord and is known now as the "father of the faithful."

Why?

Read Genesis 15:17 - 21.

God and Abram had set up an elaborate ritual to seal their covenant, something that was fairly common during Abram's day. Then just as God and Abram should have completed the ritual together, sealing the deal, God caused Abram to fall asleep, and He completed the ritual by Himself.

God knew that Abram, father of the faithful, could never be faithful enough. He knew that Abram would mess up time and time again and that his descendants would do the same. God knew of the hardships His people would have to endure as they walked beside Him. They could never hold up their end of the bargain.

So God signed the covenant with Himself. He would fulfill His promise, and He would send His Son to be the obedient Israelite, all those years later, to redeem the broken promises Abram and his descendants left behind.

Aren't you thankful for a God who doesn't need you to fulfill your end of the bargain?

Our God always breathes new life, is always good, and *He always keeps His promises.* As we walk with him, having gained righteousness in His eyes through bold faith, we will continue to miss the mark. He is never surprised when we mess up or when we get off track. But that's the beauty of life with Jesus! Sure, we can expect scary things to happen! We're human, and we live in a sinful world! But we are *completely* safe and secure in the hands of a reliable and trustworthy Father.

We love the song "Jireh" by Maverick City Music. One line in particular stands out.

"I wasn't holding You up so there's nothing I can do to let You down."[4]

From our perspective, just like Abram's perspective as He questioned God's plan, following God in faith is a crazy risk. But when we know who our God is, we see that it isn't really risky at all. We serve a God who holds up both ends of the bargain.

We could never let Him down.

So as you walk through the scary parts of life with Jesus, fix your eyes on what you know to be true. Choose faith today, maybe even for the first time in your life. Take a deep breath and take the next step into the scary, wonderful *unknown.*

THINK IT THROUGH . . .

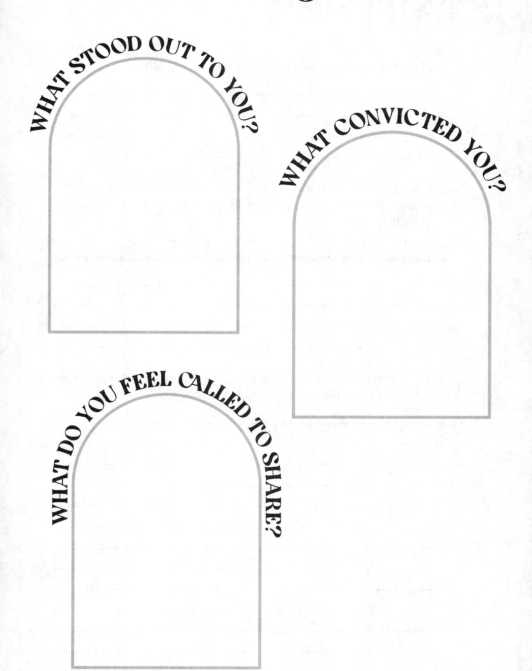

WHAT STOOD OUT TO YOU?

WHAT CONVICTED YOU?

WHAT DO YOU FEEL CALLED TO SHARE?

CONVERSATION STARTERS

+ Have you ever had to take a risky step of faith? What was it like?

_____
_____
_____
_____

+ Following God into scary moments requires a lot of trust in His character. Be honest, how would you rate your trust in Him right now? Why?

0   1   2   3   4   5   6   7   8   9   10

_____
_____
_____
_____

+ What step of faith might God be calling you to right now? What would it look like for you to step out in boldness?

_____
_____
_____
_____
_____
_____
_____
_____
_____
_____
_____

CHAPTER 4

GOD WILL DRAG YOU OUT

GENESIS
CHAPTERS 16-20

At the end of this week, we'll be almost halfway through our study of Genesis! Can you believe it? This week we are getting into the nitty gritty and studying a story that is well-known. You'll recognize that it's often quoted but for all the wrong reasons. So how can we read this famous Bible story with fresh eyes? Let's ask the Holy Spirit to reveal what God wants us to learn from the destruction of Sodom and Gomorrah. We might be surprised by how relevant it is for our own lives. To catch up, read Genesis 16 - 20 on your own. Take notes on what sticks out to you as you read or save time and take a quick peek at our chapter summaries.

LET'S REVIEW!

16 Doubting that the Lord would provide, Sarai encouraged Abram to sleep with his slave Hagar so that they could have a baby. But once Hagar became pregnant with Ishmael, tensions grew between her and Sarai. Eventually Hagar ran away. As she was running, God appeared to her and told her to go back, promising to bless her.

17 God reminded Abram of his covenant promise and cemented it even more by renaming him "Abraham" and his wife "Sarah." Then as a physical sign of His covenant, God told Abraham to circumcise all of the males in his household. Abraham obeyed.

18 God appeared to Abraham in the form of three strangers. Abraham showed the visitors his best hospitality, and they told him that by next year, Sarah would have a baby. Sarah, being nosy, was listening behind the tent curtain. She heard their pronouncement and laughed, because she was way too old to have a baby. The men got up to leave and revealed that their true purpose in coming was to destroy Sodom and Gomorrah. Abraham asked if they would spare the city if they found only ten righteous people there.

19 Angels from God then appeared to Lot, who was living right outside of Sodom. He also offered them hospitality, but the sin and craziness of the city he was camped near bled into their night, creating danger and disruption. The angels had to all but drag Lot and his family out before the whole city was destroyed.

20 Predictably, Abraham pulled the same "she is my sister" trick that he pulled in Egypt with a new king, Abimelech. And again, God intervened and rescued Sarah.

NOTES

_____
_____
_____
_____
_____
_____
_____
_____
_____
_____
_____
_____
_____
_____
_____
_____
_____
_____
_____
_____
_____
_____

 **PRAY THIS PRAYER!**

God, You are so big! I love how You can use anything for Your good and for the good of those who love You. I'm sorry for when my eyes become clouded and when I read Your Word for selfish reasons. Please give me fresh eyes as I encounter Your truth this week. Thank You for Your holy justice and Your rescuing heart. Guide me along Your path and show me how to look more like You.

GOD WILL DRAG YOU OUT

GENESIS 18:16 - 19:29

Have you ever ordered a burrito at Chipotle and loaded up on ingredients only to get to the end of the buffet line and realize that now that poor worker has to somehow fit all of that yumminess into that small, fragile-looking tortilla? It's always amazing when they miraculously manage to fold it up and seal it off.

Chapters 16 - 20 of Genesis are like the Chipotle burritos of the Bible. They are full to bursting with juicy details that you could chew on for a week straight if you wanted to. Sadly, we are going for the burrito bowl option because we have to eat quickly, but we want to encourage you to spend some time on your own in these chapters. In the meantime, here's what you missed!

+ **Use the summaries of Chapters 16 - 20 to fill in the blanks below.**

> + **Sarai told Abram to sleep with _____ and she became pregnant with a baby named _____ .**

> + **God renamed Abram and Sarai to _____ and _____ .**

> + **God told Abraham to _____ every male in his camp as a sign of the covenant.**

> + **Three men came to visit and told Abraham that Sarah was going to become _____ .**

There was obviously a lot going on for Abraham when three mysterious men showed up at his door and told him that he was going to have a baby in a year's time. And just to add to a full load of stress, Abraham was hit with another bombshell. Turns out the guac was extra.

Read Genesis 18:16 - 21.

These verses give us a cool glimpse into another character trait of God. The Lord, who we learn is one of the three men who visited Abraham, wants to share His plans with His chosen friend. We know as Christians that sharing in the plans of the Lord is a big honor that He *loves* to bestow. Check out John 15 for proof!

> "I no longer call you servants, because a servant does not know his master's business. Instead, I have called you friends, for everything that I learned from my Father I have made known to you."
> John 15:15

True to His character (as always), God decided to tell Abraham what He and His two angel buddies were in town to do.

+ What was God in town to do? (Check Genesis 18:20 - 21 for the answer.)

An outcry had reached the ears of the Lord. Just like when Abel's blood cried out from the ground when Cain killed his brother (Genesis 4), the depravity of the cities of Sodom and Gomorrah caused a cry of total distress that moved the Father to action. He was in town to check things out, but don't go thinking this was a *Scooby Doo*-type investigation. God, the ultimate deliverer of justice for the oppressed, was stepping on the scene. The mood was grim, and Abraham felt it.

Read Genesis 18:23 - 26 to see how Abraham reacted to God's news.

Abraham, like Noah before him, knew the character of God. He saw the justice that the Lord was about to deliver and decided to intercede for the people of Sodom and Gomorrah. Now it must be shocking that Abraham would find space in his heart to advocate for the people of Sodom. Didn't he already have enough on his mind?

+ Flip back to Genesis 14:12. Who might Abraham have been thinking about when he pleaded for Sodom?

Lot, Abraham's nephew, was living in Sodom. Yikes. We learned last week that Lot wasn't even supposed to be on the scene. Abraham was supposed to leave him in Haran, but he brought him along anyway. That already proved to be a bad decision (as it *always* is to go against God's commands). A few chapters ago, Abraham had to swoop in and save Lot from getting taken as a prisoner of war, and now Lot's all settled into a place that was so sinful that God had come to earth to wipe it out.

Lot was a hot mess.

With his heart clearly set on saving his beloved yet troublesome nephew, Abraham pleaded with God. We can learn a lot from his "prayer" here. He appealed to who he knew God to be while boldly asking God to stay true to His Word.

We get to see and to believe that Abraham's urgent and fervent intercession had an effect. He secured God's word that for just ten righteous people, God would spare the whole city. Surely Lot would have brought at least a few people outside of his family to the Lord in his time in Sodom, right?

The angels left Abraham, their deal done. And Abraham was confident in the rescuing heart of his God.

+ **Have you ever prayed fervently for God to help someone you loved? How might the knowledge that God wants to help them even more than you do change the way you pray for them?**

Read Genesis 19:1 - 5.

As we read on, we see that Abraham's faith in Lot may have been a bit misguided.

First, we see that Lot was sitting at the gateway of the city when the two angels came to meet him. This is not an insignificant detail. For Lot to be seated there meant that he was pretty much on the city council for Sodom[1], a confusing decision for a righteous and godly man.

+ Read 2 Peter 2:7 - 8 and take some notes on Lot's character.

Lot, despite his bad decisions, was a child of God, and he did not revel in the sin of the people he was surrounded by. But he stayed, too content in the dire circumstances to leave and far too willing to compromise his beliefs for a false feeling of safety.

It hurts to admit, but oftentimes, we are Lot in this story. We stay put even when we know that what's going on around us is wrong.

Still, Lot welcomed the visitors just like Abraham, perhaps with a little more urgency. And we quickly find out why he was so urgent to bring these visitors into his home.

"Before they had gone to bed, all the men from every part of the city of Sodom—both young and old—surrounded the house. They called to Lot, 'Where are the men who came to you tonight? Bring them out to us so that we can have sex with them.'"
Genesis 19:4 - 5

Yuck. Gross. Ew. Nasty. Creepy.

This part is so tempting to skip over, but we need to acknowledge something: These people were broken. It's no accident that the biblical authors describe this attempted sexual assault as evidence for Sodom's sin. It is the heart of pain, a deep evil.

> *If this part of the story is extra painful for you because you have personally experienced something like it, we encourage you to reach out to a trusted friend or counselor. You are not alone!*

Remember what God said?

> **"The outcry against Sodom and Gomorrah is so great and their sin so grievous . . ."**
> **Genesis 18:20b**

God wasn't exaggerating when He talked about the sin of this city. If it was at a point where *every single man* in the town came to attack Lot's guests, what else was going on in Sodom?

The part that really hurts is Lot's reaction. In verses 6 - 8, to combat the men trying to sexually assault the angel visitors, Lot actually offers his two daughters as a trade.

> **". . . you can do what you like with them."**
> **Genesis 19:8b**

We get sick to our stomach just reading this verse. Not only are we struck by the brokenness of offering two young girls in exchange for the angels, but also that Lot, a man of God, would even consider it. What would drive a man to that point? What could make a father so numb to the sinful behavior around him that he would ever view giving his two daughters up as a viable option?

Lot was used to the sin of Sodom. He had become accustomed to their practices, and he was well on his way to becoming apathetic to the horrors they participated in.

Are you used to your sin? Are you so deep in the world that it doesn't even shock you anymore?

Luckily for Lot and his family, the two angels were *not* numb to Sodom. They, with a clear display of supernatural power, saved Lot and his family from the crowd and struck all the men with blindness, "so that they could not find the door" (19:11). It's so interesting that the Bible adds in that detail. We can picture these men, young and old, so intent on the evil desires of their hearts that they are groping around in the dark, blind, trying to find the door that would lead them even deeper into their sin.

Read Genesis 19:12 - 14.

Now the angels get to business. The investigation part was over. They had seen what they needed to see. God's judgement was coming, and Lot needed to get the heck out of there. They asked Lot to find anyone in the city that "belonged to him" so that they could be saved along with him. It reminds us of Abraham's implied hope that Lot would have surely brought ten people to the Lord in his time there. Surely the others who were joining Lot's household would be desperate for escape.

Spoiler alert: They weren't. In fact, the sons-in-law actually thought that Lot was *joking*. Yikes, part two. Looks like Lot was low on credibility in his adoptive city. It seems like the residents of Sodom didn't believe God's power and certainly didn't take His judgement seriously.

The angels knew the necessary urgency and told Lot to ditch the rest of his extended household and hurry up. But what was Lot's response?

+ Copy the first three words of Genesis 19:16 in the space below.

He *hesitated*?! What?!

If you aren't frustrated with Lot yet, then props to you for your super capacity for patience. How, after watching these two "men" use their superpowers to strike a bunch of people blind, could Lot not understand that these angels meant business? How could he not see that they were from the Lord and that the destruction they warned him about was total and imminent?

But before you get too mad at Lot's dumb behavior, remember who we are in this story.

So did God strike him down right then and there for being a cowardly idiot?

+ Fill in the blanks from Genesis 19:16 below.

"When he hesitated, the men _____ _____ _____ and the hands of his wife and of his two daughters and ____ them _____ out of the city, for the LORD was _____ to them."

There it is. Right in the middle of a story that is usually used to prove God's judgement and destructive nature, we see His true character. We see His merciful and rescuing heart. While Lot was blind and fumbling, God was already chasing him down, ready to save him.

God will drag you out! Our God loves us way too much to leave us in our sin.

> **"What do you think? If a man owns a hundred sheep, and one of them wanders away, will he not leave the ninety-nine on the hills and go to look for the one that wandered off? . . . In the same way your Father in heaven is not willing that any of these little ones should perish."**
> Matthew 18:12, 14

This verse holds a popular image in the Christian world today (thanks, "Reckless Love"[2]). We all love the idea of a good Father who would leave ninety-nine beloved sheep to chase down the one who had gone astray. We like to think of ourselves as worth being chased after. We like the idea of our worth being proven in such a way. We're even okay if we aren't the lost sheep in the metaphor. We like to think of God chasing down our friend who doesn't know Him or maybe that political leader who we know "needs Jesus."

But what if that one sheep didn't want to be found?

What if that lost sheep knew exactly what she was doing when she got separated from the herd? What if she ran because she liked it better on her own or she thought that life was better outside of the protection of the Shepherd? What then?

Does she still deserve the Shepherd's singular attention? Is it still sweet and heartwarming to think about her being sought out? No! We wonder if that sheep would even appreciate being saved. She must have enjoyed being on her own, despite the very present danger. It would be better to just leave her to the consequences of her own decisions. When a predator finally got to her, it would be her own fault. Definitely not worth the Shepherd's time.

Does it hurt to know that sometimes (most of the time) we're like that ungrateful sheep?

When we are stubborn—way too comfortable in our sin to even consider allowing the Lord to refine us and rescue us from the path we chose to walk down—we are that sheep. We keep our sins on repeat, ignoring God's Word, because they aren't really that bad.

Sure, I gossip with my friends, but it's no big deal. At least I'm not being rude to anyone's face!

Yeah, I'm holding on to bitterness toward my roommate, but she will never know.

I only go to parties because my friends go, so it's not like I'm enjoying it! And when I get drunk, I never drive or do things that are dangerous.

Maybe I act like a different person when I'm around my work friends, but they would judge me for being a Christian.

It's okay for my boyfriend and I to go almost too far. We can stop whenever we want to.

We are just like Lot. We miss so many signs from God telling us that we are headed straight for destruction, because we are way too content in our current situation.

It's no big deal to live in Sodom! I'll be a good influence on them!

Why is it so easy to look at Lot's situation and see how wrong he is, but we can't look at our own and see the same?

Well God saw what was going on. He saw Lot's heart slowly becoming numb to the evil practices that were surrounding him. He saw Lot's little compromises. He saw all the times that Lot said, "Just one more time couldn't hurt."

And what did God do?

He chased after that ungrateful sheep! God didn't see Lot as a lost cause. God thought he was worth chasing down.

We read in verse 16 that the angels literally grabbed Lot's hands and dragged him out of the city. Why?

Because of God's mercy!

He didn't drag Lot out because Lot was worthy of saving or because Lot was ready to go. He dragged Lot out because Lot was in danger and God knew he needed rescue! And God will drag you out, too! He will find you in the pit when you don't even want to be found. He will shine His light so bright that it will hurt your darkness-accustomed eyes. He will grab both of your hands and pull you out even when you think you would prefer to stay down.

GOSPEL LENS

God didn't save you because you were worth saving! When God sent His only son Jesus to die on the cross for the forgiveness of your sins, it was a free gift according to God's *mercy*. We could never have saved ourselves, because we are all deep in our hopeless brokenness. But thanks to the character of our merciful God, we are called heirs to His Kingdom and beloved children.

But why make Him drag us out?

It hurts so much less to walk out with Him, hand in hand. It's so much easier to be carried to safety on your Shepherd's shoulders when you aren't kicking and screaming. You will come home with far less bruises if you don't fight Him the whole way back.

The real question is, *how do we do it?*

+ **Think of a time when God had to drag you out of your sin. How might it have been easier if you had listened to His call sooner?**

+ What pit are you sitting in right now that you know God cannot allow you to stay in? What might He be asking you to do before He has to pull you out?

Let's see how Lot's story ends.

Read Genesis 19:17 - 26.

So the Lord drags Lot out . . . kicking and screaming the whole way. You would think that God would be exasperated with Lot's childish behavior by now, but He had a promise to keep. Lot, His child, would be saved. God's character could not change.

We get a sad, little detail there at the end when Lot's wife looks back after being told not to and is turned into a pillar of salt.

Jesus even referred to this moment in His teaching; let's see how He interpreted it.

+ Find Luke 17:32 - 33 and copy it down in the space below.

The Lord had rescued His people from their broken places despite all of their whining. But for Lot's wife, that wasn't enough. She looked back, yearning for her old life. Surely those were the good ol' days? She wanted to hold on to what God had told her to let go of. And He was right to do so, because that place was poisonous to her.

What can we learn from Lot and his family? We can definitely learn not to force the Lord to drag us out. On top of that, we learn to stop looking back on our old life when we have been saved and placed on a new path.

If this all seems kinda like a downer, that's okay. It's hard not to become hopeless when we feel like we are doomed to be ungrateful sheep.

So how about this?

Aren't you thankful for a God that will drag you out?

Can you feel the relief in knowing that your God, in His mercy, is never content to leave you to the wolves?

Aren't you glad to have a Shepherd that would leave ninety-nine obedient sheep for the one rebel?

For you?

Throughout this study, we have been focusing on God's character. In fact, the whole Bible can be read as a love letter to God, a testimony to His goodness. So as we read this hard story and find ourselves connecting with Lot, it can be easy to get distracted. But, get this! *This story isn't about Lot! It's about God!*

Maybe you've never received that love in its fullness. Maybe His character is still a little fuzzy to you. What would it look like for you to accept His invitation for rescue? Maybe your sin problem, your Sodom, is really more of a passion problem. Could the biggest mountain standing in your way be a false understanding of God's character?

Lean into Him. Let Him show you His heart. Allow it to change you.

Right here, in the middle of a story full of doom and destruction, we can see hope. We can have hope that even when we are surrounded by total depravity and have both of our feet planted firmly in the wrong place, our loving, merciful, and rescuing God will chase us down and seek us out.

> **"So when God destroyed the cities of the plain, he remembered Abraham, and he brought Lot out of the catastrophe that overthrew the cities where Lot had lived."**
> **Genesis 19:29**

God remembered Abraham's desperate pleas, and He saved an unwilling man. That God remains the same today, and He will do the same for you.

Thankfully, He always keeps His promises.

THINK IT THROUGH . . .

WHAT STOOD OUT TO YOU?

WHAT CONVICTED YOU?

WHAT DO YOU FEEL CALLED TO SHARE?

CONVERSATION STARTERS

+ How does your life reflect Lot's? Have you found yourself caught up in the wrong place and hesitant to move?

_____

_____

_____

_____

_____

_____

_____

+ Why do you think you're hesitant to take God's hand as He drags you out? What is getting in the way?

_____

_____

_____

_____

_____

_____

_____

+ God thinks you are worth chasing down. Be honest, do you feel worth it? Why or why not?

_____

_____

_____

_____

_____

_____

_____

CHAPTER 5

GOD IS WORTH YOUR SACRIFICE

GENESIS
CHAPTERS 21-25

How in the world are we already halfway through Genesis? Let's just take a second to thank the Lord for the work He has been doing through this study so far! AMEN! We believe that the Word of God is alive and active (Hebrews 4:12); that has been proven *so* clearly already as we have studied the beginning of the biblical story. This week's story speaks directly to our lives as we learn how God feels about sacrifice. Take some time and read Genesis 21 - 25 and jot down some notes in the space provided. If you need the SparkNotes version this week (we get it, life can be crazy sometimes), check out the chapter summaries.

LET'S REVIEW!

21 Sarah finally gave birth to her promised son, Isaac. They threw a huge party for him, but there was (not surprisingly) tension between Sarah's son and Hagar's son. God told Abraham not to worry, so Abraham sent Hagar and Ishmael away, where the Lord provided for them just like He said He would.

22 God tested Abraham by asking him to sacrifice Isaac, his only son. Abraham obeyed and brought Isaac all the way up a mountain to make an offering. God intervened, true to His character, and provided a ram to sacrifice instead. God was proud of Abraham's obedience and blessed him.

23 Sarah died at 127 years old. After mourning his wife's death, Abraham haggled for a place to bury her. He acquired the burial land, a little piece of the Promised Land.

24 Abraham was getting old and told a servant to go find a wife for Isaac, giving him very specific instructions. The servant obeyed and found Rebekah. The servant knew that she was the one, and he asked Rebekah—with permission from her family—if she would come and be married to Isaac. Rebekah agreed, married Isaac, and he loved her.

25 Abraham died at 175 years old, and they buried him with Sarah. God blessed Isaac and Rebekah with twins after they struggled to get pregnant. The twins, Jacob and Esau, were in competition for the top spot in the family. Esau was hangry, so Jacob tricked him into selling his birthright with some bread and lentil stew.

NOTES

_____
_____
_____
_____
_____
_____
_____
_____
_____
_____
_____
_____
_____
_____
_____
_____
_____
_____
_____
_____
_____
_____
_____

 **PRAY THIS PRAYER!**

God, You are the most important. You are worth any sacrifice. I'm sorry for the moments in my life that have not reflected that belief. Thank You for every opportunity You have given me to realign my heart with Yours. Please give me fresh vision this week to see Your heart for my life.

GOD IS WORTH YOUR SACRIFICE

GENESIS 22:1 - 19

There are some Bible verses that we love to tattoo on our arms, wear on t-shirts, or put on decorative coffee mugs. These are the verses that are easy to understand and that make us feel good. But the whole Bible isn't smooth, easy reading. Some verses are harder to swallow than others.

This verse in Acts is one of the hard ones.

> "However, I consider my life worth nothing to me; my only aim is to finish the race and complete the task the Lord Jesus has given me—the task of testifying to the good news of God's grace."
> Acts 20:24

What is most important to you?

Reading Paul's words in Acts can be kind of jarring. How can life be worth nothing? It feels so wrong! But there it is, in the Bible for all of us to read:

> "... I consider my life worth nothing to me ..."
> Acts 20:24b

Paul was a man of great faith. He had a dramatic encounter with the Savior, and his whole life changed. He became dedicated to sharing the Good News to everyone he possibly could. This guy even wrote a good chunk of the New Testament! So how in the *world* could he have considered his life . . .

Meaningless?

Worthless?

Nothing?

Let's look at it again.

+ What does Paul consider to have worth according to this verse?

The only thing worth his time and attention was the good news of God's grace.

And no one could even try to debate him, because his life proved his belief!

This man was shipwrecked, jailed, stoned, and suffered great persecution *all for the name of Jesus*. It looks like Paul had decided that God was the most important thing to him; the only important thing.

Could we ever make that same decision?

As we continue on in Abraham's story, we see that he had to face that choice: God or everything else that was important to him. Let's see how he responded.

Read Genesis 22:1 - 2.

Things go from zero to one hundred real quick. The only intro we get here is "some time later," and then it goes straight into human sacrifice. At this point in Genesis, though, we aren't even surprised.

This book is *wild*.

But if you have been reading closely, this beginning might feel a little confusing since the last time we talked about Abraham, he was childless. Let's fill in the gaps!

+ Find Genesis 21:1 - 5 and summarize it in your own words.

Abraham and Sarah finally got their promised son! This kid, Isaac, was the culmination of all of their most fervent prayers! The blessing they had desperately prayed for was finally here. And not only was it a fulfillment of this old married couple's dreams, but it was a big step in God's covenant with Abraham.

> "As for me, this is my covenant with you: You will be the father of many nations."
> Genesis 17:4

Abraham must have felt like things were finally coming together. His life was finally on the right track. Then *boom*, God delivered a bombshell.

+ Fill in the blanks from Genesis 22:2.

"Then God said, 'Take your son, your only son, _____ ____ _____— Isaac—and go to the region of Moriah. _____ him there as a burnt offering on a mountain I will show you."

Hardcore. Let's clear some things up first.

Read 2 Kings 16:3.

+ Does God condone human sacrifice (circle your answer)?

Yes   No

No! Though human and child sacrifice was sadly a fairly common practice in the region where Abraham lived, it was something that was detestable to God. So we can bookmark that verse to prove His character. And knowing who God is, we can read a verse like Genesis 22:2 and be appropriately shocked.

Why is God asking Abraham to do something He doesn't approve of?

Abraham had a lot of ups and downs in his life and faith walk, but by this moment, near the end of his life (he dies in three chapters), he really was living up to his title as the "father of the faithful." We see it in his eager "Here I am" in verse 22 and, as we continue to read, his response to God's command. This test from God really wasn't to produce more faith in Abraham. Instead, it was to reveal the faith God had already planted in him.[1]

So we know that God was asking for something He didn't agree with and that Abraham was being tested. The third important thing to remember is our favorite, because it's about Jesus.

+ Fill in the blanks from Romans 8:32.

"He who did not spare ____ ____ ____, but gave him up for us all—how will he not also, along with him, graciously give us all things?"

Are you seeing the similarities between Abraham's story and the story of Jesus? It's okay if you aren't yet, because there are more connection points coming. But what is important to know is that God Himself gave up His only son, just like He was asking Abraham to do here. If you want to impress everyone with your theological knowledge, here's a fun tidbit! Biblical scholars call the sacrifice of Isaac a *prophetic reenactment.*[2] That's just a fancy way of saying that when we read that God asked Abraham to sacrifice Isaac, it's supposed to remind us of what Jesus did on the cross (think John 3:16). We'll talk more about this later, so keep it in your back pocket for now.

Read Genesis 22:3 - 5.

Whoa! Abraham really is an example of faithfulness. He found out that he had to kill his only son, and how did he respond?

> **"... Abraham got up and loaded his donkey."**
> Genesis 22:3b

Don't you want to be that quick to obey? We can all probably think of times in our lives when we felt a nudge from the Lord, then spent three months wrestling with it, begging for confirmation, and talking it through with everyone we know. Abraham heard from the Lord and woke up early the next morning to obey.

+ **Have you ever delayed obedience to the Lord? Describe your situation below. What would it look like for you to be quick to obey like Abraham?**

So our boy Abe packed up, brought Isaac along, and set out to the place God had told him about. Then after a symbolic three days (hint: Jesus), he said something strange.

+ **Record what Abraham says to his servants in verse 5.**

Ummm . . . that's weird! Why would Abraham say that they both would return if he knew that Isaac was going to die?

+ Take a guess at why Abraham would say that in the space below, even if you aren't sure.

It seems that either Abraham didn't think that Isaac would die or he was sugar coating things for the sake of his company. Lots of things in the Bible are ambiguous and intentionally left unclear so that we can wrestle with God and seek His understanding, but luckily, this isn't one of those moments.

Check out what Hebrews says about this instance in Genesis!

> "By faith Abraham, when God tested him, offered Isaac as a sacrifice. He who had embraced the promises was about to sacrifice his one and only son, even though God had said to him, 'It is through Isaac that your offspring will be reckoned.' Abraham reasoned that God could even raise the dead, and so in a manner of speaking he did receive Isaac back from death."
> **Hebrews 11:17 - 19**

That came from left field! We're assuming you didn't guess that Abraham actually believed that God was going to resurrect Isaac, but if you did, props to you for your elite Bible knowledge. When we think about it in light of the full biblical story, it kind of makes sense. We know that God does raise people from the dead (Jesus, along with others), so it's not crazy for Abraham to assume that. But get this! At this point in Scripture, God hadn't raised *anyone* from the dead! Abraham had no precedent for this belief! So why would he assume God would resurrect Isaac when He had never done something like that before?

Abraham trusted that God would always be true to His word.

In Genesis 21:12, God told Abraham that it would be through Isaac that the covenant would be fulfilled. Abraham took God at His word and believed that what He said was true. Now when everything suddenly got difficult and heartbreaking, Abraham was holding on to God's promise.

Next we watch as Abraham and Isaac head up the mountain. Isaac noticed that they don't have a lamb for the burnt offering, and he asked his dad about it.

+ **Fill in the blanks from Abraham's answer in Genesis 22:8b.**

"God himself will _____ the _____ for the burnt offering, my son."

Is the Jesus imagery coming into clearer focus for you? How cool is it that we can see signs of our Savior all the way back in Genesis?!

Read Genesis 22:9 - 13.

We have finally hit the climax of the story. Abraham, in complete obedience and trust

Jesus is often referred to as the "Lamb of God" (John 1:29). In this story, we can see why. Because of the sin and brokenness of the world, sacrifice is required for forgiveness. Think of it like a necessary blood price, a cost for sin. Before Jesus, Jewish people would sacrifice animals like lambs as atonement for their sins, and God would accept it as payment. But Jesus came to earth for us and died as the ultimate and final sacrifice for all of our sins: past, present, and future. He was the lamb that came straight from the Lord. As Abraham believed all those years before, God really would provide the Lamb.

in God's promise, prepared to go through with the sacrifice. He got to the point where he was actively swinging his knife to slay his precious son when an angel of the Lord stopped him.

"Abraham! Abraham!"

Abraham, the picture of obedience, answered the call.

"Here I am."

Abraham was open and ready to follow the voice of the Lord wherever it led, regardless of what he might have to lose. But God, always true to His character, revealed His heart.

> "'Do not lay a hand on the boy,' he said. 'Do not do anything to him. Now I know that you fear God, because you have not withheld from me your son, your only son.'"
> Genesis 22:12

Here we finally get to understand what God was up to. We finally see the answer to our "why?" question from earlier.

God was reminding Abraham that He was worth his sacrifice.

When we talk about this story, it's often referred to as "the Sacrifice of Isaac," but the important part about this story, the part that is most remarkable, is that *God did not want Isaac to die*![3] He never planned to kill off Isaac! His plan was for Abraham. He wanted to remind Abraham of his priorities. He wanted Abraham to prove his devotion to God above all else.

Think about it! Abraham had prayed for almost a century for a son. This was his deepest desire, the thing closest to his heart. But, as we know, the things that we desire most are the things that are in the most danger of being idolized and placed in a position of honor *above God*!

119

Our God is not content with second place.

Yes, Isaac was a beautiful gift from God, but he wasn't God. Isaac wasn't created to hold the place of supreme affection in Abraham's heart, and God knew it. So God reminded Abraham of what mattered most to him. When he placed Isaac on the altar, Abraham chose God over God's gift.

Is God the most important thing in your life?

Think about your day to day life. Where do you spend your time? Where do you spend your energy? What holds your heart? What dream is most tied to your identity?

HARD TRUTH TIME!

+ **Be honest, where does God lie on your list of priorities?**

| HONESTLY, HE ISN'T A PRIORITY FOR ME. | HE GETS SOME OF MY TIME BUT NOT A LOT. | GOD IS IMPORTANT TO ME, BUT SOMETIMES HE GETS PUSHED LOWER ON THE LIST. | I ACTIVELY CHOOSE THE LORD OVER OTHER THINGS. | GOD IS MY #1 ALL THE TIME! |

+ **Take some time and write down the things in your life (relationships, hobbies, hopes, passions, responsibilities). Rank them in order of which gets the most time and attention. Where is God ranked on our list?**

What changes might He be calling you to make to realign your priorities?

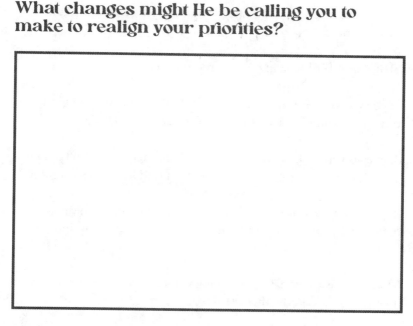

Our lives are filled with *so* many good gifts from the Lord! Friendships, grades, and even dreams are important and can be incredibly life-giving, but when we elevate these things over the Lord, our lives can get out of whack. We were created to function with complete dependence on God. When we try to depend on other things to fill us up, we will always end up empty and searching.

That's why God, in His goodness, asks you to put your life on the altar. Think about it as a reset button for life. God wants to remind you what you really value. He wants to put you back on the right path, the path where you can thrive.

Abraham's greatest desire, his biggest dream for his life, was fulfilled in Isaac. To be that boy's father was everything he ever wanted. What is your biggest dream? What would happen if God asked you to lay it down? If your heart hurts just thinking about it, maybe you have tied too much of your identity to who you want to be instead of whose you already are. Maybe Abraham was going down that same path. God knew what he needed, and God knows what you need.

What might He be asking you to put on the altar?

Maybe you have elevated your grades above Him, and you get all of your worth and identity from A's instead of from God.

Maybe you are so busy with your social life that time with God gets pushed to the few stolen minutes you can find in between activities.

Maybe you have this plan for your life that you hold so desperately to, but sometimes you wonder how you would react if it didn't come true.

Whatever it is for you, God is asking you to trust in His promises. He wants you to know that He is worth your sacrifice.

Let's take this even further. Okay, maybe God hasn't highlighted a specific thing in your life that you need to put on the altar, but that doesn't mean you are exempt from this conversation. We all need to lay it *all* down at the feet of Jesus. We get to surrender everything in our lives to Him, believing that He is in control and that He will make everything work according to His purpose.

Only through surrender are we able to look at our lives like Paul did. We give up all that "nothing," and we gain everything.

When Abraham put Isaac—his dearly loved son—on the altar, the Lord gave him back! Isaac didn't need to die! We aren't saying you need to drop everything in your life and move to a nunnery. What we are saying is that, maybe you need to be reminded of where your priorities lie.

Let's finish up our story.

In the end, God provided the necessary sacrifice. He told Abraham that because of his proven obedience, because of his willingness to sacrifice, God would bless him (verses 15 - 18).

Now that's something that is hard to wrap our minds around. How can sacrifice be a blessing?

In the act of sacrifice, something has to die. But through that death, something else is given the chance at new life. Think about Jesus's sacrifice for us! God solved the problem of death, not by condemning all of us to die the way we deserved but by offering Himself! Jesus's sacrifice, though heartbreaking because of His complete innocence, gave us all the opportunity for new life![4]

The cool thing about life with our God is that we are always getting more than we give. When we sacrifice, it's not just a legalistic proof of our nominal affiliation with the "Christian club." Our sacrifice is a beautiful expression of our affection for the most worthy King. And when we give Him that gift, what we receive in return is a million times more precious than what we gave up in the first place.

> "Then [Jesus] said to them all: 'Whoever wants to be my disciple must deny themselves and take up their cross daily and follow me. For whoever wants to save their life will lose it, but whoever loses their life for me will save it."
> Luke 9:23 - 24

This week, take a look at your life. What is God calling you to put on the altar? Maybe your sacrifice will be the key to unlocking new life.

THINK IT THROUGH...

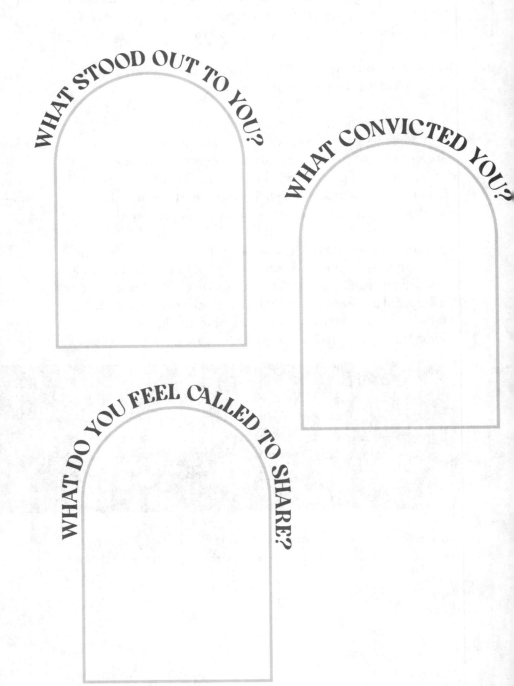

WHAT STOOD OUT TO YOU?

WHAT CONVICTED YOU?

WHAT DO YOU FEEL CALLED TO SHARE?

CONVERSATION STARTERS

+ If you're being honest, what is your top priority right now?

_____
_____
_____
_____

+ Think of a time when you had to make a sacrifice but it led to something better. What was that experience like?

_____
_____
_____
_____
_____
_____

+ What would it look like for you to lay your whole life on the altar? What is God calling you to lay at His feet?

_____
_____
_____
_____
_____
_____
_____
_____
_____
_____

CHAPTER 6

GOD SEES YOU

GENESIS
CHAPTERS 26-30

Here's a hot take for you: Genesis is hard to relate to. This book is just so ancient! It's all about goats and polygamy, and to be honest, most of the time it's hard to understand how it could be relevant to life in the United States of America in the year 2022. But just because it's difficult doesn't mean that we should just give up and assume we could never understand. Because if we did that, we would miss stories like what happens in Genesis 29: boy drama.

You know that feeling you get when you're Snapping a guy who definitely Snaps ten other girls at the same time? The women in our story this week can relate to that feeling. Read Genesis 26 - 30 on your own and take notes. As always, we have some summaries for you to skim over if you need them or don't have time to read.

LET'S REVIEW!

26 God reaffirmed to Isaac His promise of blessing Abraham's descendents, although Isaac was just as misguided as his father. He even pulled the same "she's not my wife" trick with Rebekah. Nevertheless, the Lord blessed Isaac and his family, helping them to thrive.

27 When Isaac was old, Rebekah and Jacob made a plot to steal Esau's blessing. They tricked Isaac into blessing Jacob instead, and it worked. Esau was so mad that Rebekah told Jacob to run away for his own safety.

28 As Jacob was escaping his brother's anger, the Lord appeared to him in a dream of a stairway to heaven. In this dream, God shared the family covenant with Jacob, promising to bless him and to give his offspring the Promised Land.

29 As Jacob continued on his journey, he came to a well, ran into Rachel, and immediately fell in love. Jacob agreed to work for seven years under Laban, Rachel's dad, in order to marry her. But when he had done that, Laban tricked him and gave Jacob Rachel's older sister, Leah, instead. Outraged but still hopelessly in love with Rachel, Jacob agreed to work another seven years for her. Even though Jacob loved Rachel more, the Lord was with Leah and gave her many children.

30 As having too many wives tends to do, lots of baby drama ensued within Jacob's family. Leah had lots of kids but Rachel couldn't, so Jacob slept with Rachel's slave, but, not to be outdone, Leah also gave *her* slave to Jacob to sleep with. Rachel eventually had a baby of her own and named him Joseph. To add to the drama, the success of Jacob's herds began to threaten Laban, so tensions grew between them.

NOTES

_____
_____
_____
_____
_____
_____
_____
_____
_____
_____
_____
_____
_____
_____
_____
_____
_____
_____
_____
_____
_____
_____
_____

 **PRAY THIS PRAYER!**

God, You are worthy of all of my praise, all of my love, and all of my attention. I'm sorry for searching everywhere else for the love only You can give. Thank You for watching me, caring for me, and taking delight in me. Please help me to see Your hands at work in my life.

GOD SEES YOU

GENESIS 29:15 - 30:24

Here at Delight, we try not to talk about boys. Really!

This is a *women's* ministry! We don't want to be the ministry that only talks about boys. That was never the plan! We want to be the ministry that only talks about Jesus! So we try to avoid the boy talk when we can.

But sometimes we need some boy talk. Sometimes it's good for the soul. Let's face it, we all have some boy drama in our lives, whether it's in the past or way too current. And it's so easy to blame it on them . . .

Boys are stupid!

He played me!

I don't need no man!

But isn't blaming the guys just giving them the power? Isn't it just telling them that they have control over our situations?

Maybe we can talk about our boy drama in a better way. It's not "boy drama" any more. It's our own *heart drama*. When we get hurt in a relationship, when we get rejected, and even when we get totally passed over by a guy we thought was the one, our reactions can sometimes reflect the state of our hearts.

So really, this is between us and God. We are meant to be *His* bride. He should be our one focus, our one source of affection, affirmation, and worth. What do we do when we aren't feeling that? What do we do when our boy problems—or heart problems—bring us to rock bottom?

We refocus on God. *Who is He, and what does that mean for us?*

In Genesis 29 and 30, we see some major boy problems happening.

Oops, sorry. We see some major *heart problems* happening.

As we read Leah's story, try looking for the character of God instead of focusing on the mess. When she felt rejected, alone, and unloved, how did her Lord respond?

Read Genesis 29:15 - 18.

We're confused already. Let's go back for some context.

+ Who is Jacob (See Genesis 25:19 - 26 for the answer)?

It looks like we have skipped ahead in our narrative. After weeks of focusing on Abraham's life story, now we zoom in on the life of one of his grandsons, Jacob.

Jacob was one of the twin sons of Isaac, the guy who survived the almost-sacrifice from last week. Jacob's slightly older—but much hairier—brother was Esau. But none of that answers why Jacob was staying with this random dude, Uncle Laban, instead of with his immediate family.

+ Check out Genesis 27:41 - 45. Why did Jacob have to leave?

Jacob tricked his dad into giving him the blessing that belonged to the firstborn, and Esau was understandably upset. Jacob's mom advised him to run for his life.

This family had some issues.

Flash forward, and we are back to Genesis 29. Jacob ended up staying with Laban, who apparently had two eligible daughters.

+ Check out the descriptions of Laban's daughters in Genesis 29:16 - 17. Take some notes below.

LEAH   RACHEL

Ummm . . . did the Bible just say that Rachel was hot and Leah wasn't? Seriously?

The NIV translation describes Leah as having "weak eyes." Scholars aren't really sure what this means. Some argue that she literally couldn't see very well or that maybe her eyes were "dull," while Rachel's were beautiful and glowing. Regardless, it's a very clear comparison between two sisters. One was beautiful and worth attention while the other was not.[1]

What an intro.

We learn that Laban wanted Jacob to stay and work for him, and they agreed on a form of payment.

+ Fill in the blanks from Genesis 29:18 on Jacob's agreed upon payment.

"Jacob was in love with _____ and said, 'I'll work for you _____ years in return for your younger daughter _____.'"

Let's go ahead and start addressing this elephant in the room, because there will be more. It is straight up *gross* that Laban was selling his daughter into marriage as payment for Jacob's labor. Unfortunately, that wasn't an uncommon thing in that day and age. That doesn't mean it isn't nasty, but let's keep moving.

So Jacob had the hots for Rachel and was in love with her, maybe for her sexy bod or maybe they were actually soul mates. We don't know. Regardless, he worked for seven years, but it all felt worth it to him.

"So Jacob served seven years to get Rachel, but they seemed like only a few days to him because of his love for her."
Genesis 29:20

Awww. This is starting to feel like a Disney movie. How cute! The boy is about to get the girl!

Read Genesis 29:21 - 27.

Definitely not a Disney movie.

The wedding came and Laban gave Jacob a taste of his own medicine. Jacob the player got played. But this was a little more dramatic than an episode of *Punk'd* with Ashton Kutcher. Laban tricked Jacob into marrying Leah instead of Rachel.

Yeah, we know this is a lot to unpack.

First of all, how the heck was it possible for Jacob not to realize that he was marrying the wrong girl? You'd think it would be pretty obvious! Well, Leah was likely wearing a thick veil throughout the wedding ceremonies. In fact, the only time she would have taken it off would be for the sex part, which—as could be easily arranged by sneaky Laban—was likely in the dark.

The next question in your head is probably, *Why would Leah agree to this?* We hate to break it to you, but the ancient cultures were not as girl power-motivated as we are today. Leah probably didn't have a choice.

But there's a chance that she did. What if she agreed to her father's plan, because she secretly loved Jacob? Or what if she thought that no one would ever marry her willingly? Whatever was going on in her head, it was definitely heart drama.

So the wedding happened and Jacob woke up next to the wrong woman.

Naturally, he was mad.

> **"What is this you have done to me? I served you for Rachel, didn't I? Why have you deceived me?"**
> **Genesis 29:25b**

Laban, unperturbed, gave a lame excuse about the sisters' ages, then came up with a new plan.

+ **Fill in the blanks from Laban's new plan in Genesis 29:27.**

"Finish this daughter's bridal week; then we will give you the _____ ____ _____ , in return for another _____ _____ of work."

Okayyyyy. Polygamy. Let's discuss.

Genesis has lots of instances where a man takes more than one wife. So we gotta know whether God is down for all this extra wifing. Let's do some digging.

+ **Copy Genesis 2:24 in the space below.**

According to Genesis 2, God's original plan was for a man and his wife to become one in flesh. That sounds like a pretty exclusive club. You can't go around becoming one in flesh with every lady you see! So if that was the ideal, how did we get to polygamy?

+ **Find Genesis 2:19 - 24. Who is the first guy to have more than one wife?**

Lamech was the OG polygamist. He was also murderous and bloodthirsty.

So does God like polygamy? Nope! We don't think so! But that doesn't mean He can't use it. In fact, in the specific instance of polygamy in Jacob's case, it ended up producing twelve sons who later became the twelve tribes of Israel.

But if you have ever seen an episode of *Sister Wives*, you know that sharing a husband *always* leads to drama.

Let's jump back into the story.

Jacob finished Leah's bridal week, then immediately married his true love, Rachel. This section of the story ends on a somber note, especially for Leah.

> "Jacob made love to Rachel also, and his love for Rachel was greater than his love for Leah. And he worked for Laban another seven years."
> Genesis 29:30

Jacob loved Rachel more than he loved Leah. But let's not focus on Jacob right now, even though he definitely has a lot of problems going on. What does this all mean for Leah?

Put yourself in her shoes. She got married, one of the biggest accomplishments a woman was allowed to achieve in her culture. Jacob was probably a hunk. He's this mysterious guy who just showed up one day on the family farm. Maybe Leah really did love him. Maybe she thought he could love her back. Then, after the wedding and after she gave herself to him in the most intimate way, he woke up and told everyone he wanted her sister more. Not only did he announce that, but he actually went and married her the very next week.

Leah was, without a doubt, experiencing some heart drama. Maybe calling it drama is trivializing it; Leah was in deep pain.

Where is God in all this? How could He allow Jacob and Laban to hurt Leah like this?

Read Genesis 29:31 - 34.

+ **Fill in the blanks from Genesis 29:31.**

"When the LORD _____ that Leah was not _____, he enabled her to conceive, but Rachel remained childless."

The Lord *saw* Leah in her pain.

Leah, by all accounts, is a minor character in this story. It's easier to notice Jacob and his passionate love for Rachel or Laban and his craftiness. But the Lord didn't take notice of the ones who were the easiest to see. He saw Leah. He saw the girl who was unloved, picked over, and ugly to the world. He saw her in her pain and decided to take action. He decided to step in and join her in her sadness.

+ **Have you ever felt unseen? How does it make you feel to know that your God sees you in your pain?**

So God decided to swoop in and helped Leah have lots of babies, effectively making her the more "valuable" wife.

+ Record the name and meaning of Leah's first son below (verse 32).

Leah realized that this first kid, Reuben, was a gift from the Lord. But her thoughts were hinting at what must have been going on in her heart.

"Surely my husband will love me now."
Genesis 29:32b

Leah recognized that God stepped in for her, but she missed His heart, the tone of compassion in the gift. She thought that, because of Reuben, Jacob was bound to love her now.

Leah was chasing the heart of Jacob instead of the heart of God.

Have you ever done that? Have you ever been so desperate for a boy's attention, approval, or affection that everything you did was for him? Have you ever begged God to make someone like you just so you wouldn't have to be lonely anymore?

Maybe boy drama isn't your thing. So think about it this way: Have you ever been desperate for the approval of your parents? Have you ever wanted to be the favorite friend, chosen first in the friend group?

We are all craving attention. We all want to be loved. So what happens when the world can't give us what we need?

Well, how did Leah react?

+ Record the name and meaning of Leah's second son below (verse 33).

God, ever patient, sent Leah another token of His affection. He sent her these gifts almost as signposts.

I love you, Leah! I see you, Leah!

But Leah's eyes were still focused on the wrong man.

> **"Because the LORD heard that I am not loved, he gave me this one too."**
> **Genesis 29:33b**

Leah saw Simeon as but another reminder that she was unloved when, really, he was a gift from a God who loved her more than she could ever imagine. She viewed this gift as pity from God, instead of as a token of His affection. All she was thinking about was Jacob's attention.

Then, a third son was born to her. You know the drill by now.

+ Record the name and meaning of Leah's third son below (verse 34).

At this point in the chapter, Leah is almost incredulous. How could Jacob not love her now? She had done so much to earn his attention! How could three sons not be enough?

> **"Now at last my husband will become attached to me."**
> **Genesis 29:34b**

Leah had the wrong goal in mind. She was so desperate to earn the affection and preference of Jacob that she missed the unearned and freely given love that God was showering on her.

Sadly, we do the same thing. We have this tunnel vision in our lives, hoping desperately for a fairytale ending with a hot guy who falls in the perfect place between a dad bod and washboard abs. We focus so hard on that outcome and that "prize" that we miss the delight that our heavenly Father takes in us.

> **"He brought me out into a spacious place; he rescued me because he delighted in me."**
> **Psalm 18:19**

HARD TRUTH TIME!

+ Be honest, do you see yourself as worthy of God's love?

HE COULD NEVER LOVE SOMEONE LIKE ME.	HE WILL LOVE ME MORE ONCE I GET MY ACT TOGETHER.	MAYBE HE THINKS ABOUT ME.	I KNOW THAT I AM CHOSEN BY GOD.	I AM 100% SURE THAT THE LORD LOVES ME UNCONDITIONALLY.

+ Think about it, whose attention, approval, and affirmation is most important to you right now? Why?

Our girl Leah was trying so hard to earn Jacob's love and attention, when she had God's the whole time.

So what finally got through to her?

+ Record the name and meaning of Leah's fourth son below (verse 35).

"This time I will praise the LORD."
Genesis 29:35b

Finally Leah shifted her focus. She turned her face to the Lord's and saw Him for what He was, worthy of her praise.

God was with Leah the whole time, even when she didn't see Him there. He had always seen her, even when she felt unseen. If that was His character then, that is His character now.

He sees you. He sees you when you feel unloved, not chosen, and totally unseen. And not only does He *see* you, but He *loves* you! In fact, He loves you so much that He sent His son to die for you, just to prove His affection.

Let's finish up this story.

Spoiler alert, God eventually gave Rachel children, too. And there was all this drama about whose servant could have the most sons with Jacob, so obviously Leah and Rachel were not over their sisterly competition. But God used all of that babymaking for His purposes. Remember what we learned at the beginning of this week? The twelve tribes of Israel were named after Jacob's sons! They were another step in the fulfillment of God's promise

GOSPEL LENS

Do you know the story of Jesus and the woman at the well? It's this moment where Jesus revealed Himself as the Messiah to a Samaritan woman by proving that He *knew* her. The woman ran into town saying, "Come, see a man who told me everything I ever did. Could this be the Messiah?" (John 4:29). What convinced this woman that Jesus was God was that He *saw* her, clearer than she had ever been seen before. Jesus, your Savior, sees you, too. He wants to prove how special you are to Him. All it takes is one conversation.

to Abraham! God continues to bless and work through His chosen people, even when they are a hot mess.

"The nation of Israel is born out of family dysfunction, which will be with them throughout their existence."[2]

So what about Leah? Where's the silver lining in her story? Yes, God saw her in her pain, but why did she have to endure the pain in the first place?

Leah, despite her neglect, had a great purpose in God's plan. Levi and Judah, two of her sons, became two of the most important tribes of Israel (the priestly tribe and the royal tribe). And looking even further, guess who else came from Leah's line?

Jesus Christ, Savior of the world.

Yup, our Messiah came from the less attractive and unseen sister.[3]

Aren't you glad to serve a God who sees you? A God who chooses to use the unlikely?

Next time you get caught up in boy drama or are in need of straight up heart surgery, remember where your help comes from.

He wants to show you just how much He loves you.

THINK IT THROUGH . . .

WHAT STOOD OUT TO YOU?

WHAT CONVICTED YOU?

WHAT DO YOU FEEL CALLED TO SHARE?

CONVERSATION STARTERS

+ Leah had all of her attention on Jacob instead of on God. What are some things that take your attention off of the Lord?

_____

_____

_____

_____

+ Have you ever felt unseen? What was it like?

_____

_____

_____

_____

_____

_____

_____

_____

_____

_____

+ Do you need to be reminded that your God delights in you? Take some time to find a Bible verse that shows His love for you, like Psalm 18:19. Write your verse below and take some time this week to memorize it.

_____

_____

_____

_____

_____

_____

CHAPTER 7

GOD IS IN THE STRUGGLE

GENESIS

CHAPTERS 31-35

This week we get to talk about something that is a little bit taboo in Christian circles. It's probably not something your grandma would approve of discussing in Bible study (sorry, Granny). This week we are talking about doubt. As Christians, admitting to doubt in our faith lives makes us feel "less than" and dirty. If faith is our basis, our solid rock to stand on, how are we supposed to act when that faith gets questioned or feels challenged? Thankfully, we have a God who likes to get down in the mud and join us as we struggle. To jump in, go ahead and read Genesis 31 - 35. You will definitely need the extra context this week! Check out the summaries below for an overview.

LET'S REVIEW!

31 Because of the rising tension with Laban, Jacob decided to pack up his family and herds and leave. Laban was upset when he found out that they left in secret, but he and Jacob eventually parted ways on good terms. But not until after Rachel stirred up extra drama by stealing some of her father's household idols.

32 As they prepared to pass into Esau's territory, Jacob got really worried. He remembered Esau's anger against him and begged God to keep them safe. He made an elaborate plan to try to appease Esau and split his family up to set it in motion. When Jacob was alone, he wrestled with God (literally) and asked Him for a blessing.

33 When Jacob finally met up with Esau, he was welcomed by his brother with open arms, not angry like he was expecting Esau to be. Esau ran and hugged Jacob, making all of his anxious preparations seem silly.

34 Settling near Shechem turned out to be a bad idea when Jacob's daughter Dinah was raped. The men begged Jacob to give her to them for marriage, but Jacob's sons were outraged, of course, at the mistreatment of their sister. They tricked the men of Shechem and ended up killing them all and plundering the city.

35 God helped Jacob and his family purify themselves and reset after the horror of the Shechem situation. He reaffirmed His covenant with them at Bethel and renamed Jacob "Israel." Rachel had one last son, Benjamin, and died in labor. This brought Israel's sons to a total of twelve. Israel visited his father Isaac with Esau, and they were with him when he died.

NOTES

_____

_____

_____

_____

_____

_____

_____

_____

_____

_____

_____

_____

_____

_____

_____

_____

_____

_____

_____

_____

_____

_____

_____

_____

 **PRAY THIS PRAYER!**

I love You, Lord! Even when I can't see it, I know that You
are working. I'm sorry for getting weighed down by all of my
questions, doubts, and insecurities. I believe, but help my unbelief.
Thank You for Your endless grace. Please show me how to step even
deeper into my faith. I want to choose You all the time.

GOD IS IN THE STRUGGLE

GENESIS 32:22 - 32

Have you ever heard the story of doubting Thomas? It's this story from the book of John where one of Jesus's disciples refused to believe the other guys' word that Jesus had really risen from the dead.

> **"But he said to them, 'Unless I see the nail marks in his hands and put my finger where the nails were, and put my hand into his side, I will not believe.'"**
> John 20:25b

Eventually Jesus showed up to set him straight. He held out His hands and told Thomas to touch Him, proving that He actually had come back to life after His brutal crucifixion. Thomas finally believed and the section ends with these words from Jesus:

> **Because you have seen me, you have believed; blessed are those who have not seen and yet have believed."**
> John 20:29b

It seems like we're always taught this story as a cautionary tale. We are *not* supposed to be like doubting Thomas. We are supposed to be like those blessed people who believe without seeing.

But what do we do if we *are* Thomas? Or better yet, what would Jesus do if we were Thomas?

Read that Scripture again. Jesus, knowing Thomas's doubts, decided to show up for him. He met him in the middle of his uncertainty and held His hands out to him.

> **"Put your finger here; see my hands. Reach out your hand and put it into my side. Stop doubting and believe."**
> **John 20:27b**

We might all be scared of Thomas's doubt. We might all use it as a horror story, something to scare away those crazy doubters.

But that's not what Jesus did.

Jesus met Thomas in his questioning and gave him exactly what he needed, and He will do the same for us!

And even crazier, He did the same thing for Jacob all the way back in Genesis.

Wait! Jesus showed up in Genesis? What?

Strap in, ladies! Things are about to get wild!

Read Genesis 32:22 - 32.

An alternate name for this chapter could be "God, Pro Wrestler." What the heck is happening here? How did we get here from last week's polygamy fiasco?

Let's fill in some missing context!

Jacob, as usual, was in a bit of a pickle. He escaped from Laban in the dead of night, stealing away his herds and his family, because he heard from the Lord in a dream that it was time to head back to the land of his relatives. But he quickly figured out that the grass wasn't necessarily greener on the other side. Even though it had been twenty years since he had seen Esau, Jacob was terrified that his brother was still mad about the trickery he had done all those years ago. Here in chapter 32, Jacob is gearing up to reunite with him.

The thing is that Jacob was freaking out. He was scheming and planning, desperately trying to come up with a plan that would result in an amicable meeting with Esau. Verse 9 reveals where his stress may have been coming from.

+ Copy down the first three words from Genesis 32:9 below.

```



```

"Then Jacob prayed." Looks like asking God for guidance was an afterthought for him. It definitely wasn't his first response. He was so caught up in his frantic planning that talking to the Lord was just another thing to check off the list.

This man needed a reset. Had he forgotten that God had called him to go home in the first place? He was overplanning and over preparing, because he wasn't sure that God would come through.

Jacob, the doubter.

Just like He did with Thomas, God knew exactly what Jacob needed. The first step was to get rid of all distractions. God wanted Jacob alone for this meeting. Jacob sent everyone off ahead of him, finally taking some time to just stop and be still.

+ Rewrite Genesis 32:24 in the space below.

Jacob was alone, and a man wrestled with him all night. (Spoiler alert, that man was God.)

+ Go back to the verse you copied down and circle the word "alone." God needed to get Jacob alone for the reset and the wrestling. Are you ever alone with God? What would it look like for you to make time to just sit with Him?

So God and Jacob were wrestling, and the Bible says that God, "saw that he could not overpower him" (verse 25). Let's clarify this!

God could overpower him. He is all powerful, after all! And we even see that He magically dislocated Jacob's hip with a touch in the same verse, so why did the author even add in the "couldn't overpower him" part?

We think that we are supposed to see here that Jacob was persistent. He was literally on the ground with God, wrestling for his life. They were at it all night! But Jacob didn't give up.

When we wrestle with God, maybe with doubts or questions, our temptation is to just throw in the towel. How many friends do you have who used to be Christians, but they encountered a hard place and decided that faith wasn't for them? We are called to be like Jacob, to keep wrestling through the night, even when it doesn't make sense.

Think about it, maybe Jacob thought he could win. He really was pushing through for some kind of victory over God. He wanted to be right. So why would God allow it to continue? He could have turned the tide at any moment, like He did with the hip thing. God was always going to win! Why did He let it go on for so long?

There must have been purpose in the struggle.

Ahhhh. Now it's starting to make a little more sense.

Read Genesis 32:26 - 29 again.

The man (God) asked persistent little Jacob to let him go. But what did Jacob say to that?

+ Write Jacob's response to God in the space below (verse 26b).

```
┌─────────────────────────────────────────────┐
│                                               │
│                                               │
│                                               │
│                                               │
└─────────────────────────────────────────────┘
```

Jacob wasn't leaving until he got a blessing. He recognized that this man he was wrestling with was more than human (the mystical hip socket wrenching might have been a giveaway), and he didn't want to leave empty handed. Jacob, having wrestled so hard for so long, was finally at the point where all he could do was hold on to the Lord with everything he had.[1]

The book of Hosea actually gives us more context for what this moment looked like. Check out this verse:

> "In the womb he grasped his brother's heel; as a man he struggled with God. He struggled with the angel and overcame him; he wept and begged for his favor."
> Hosea 12:3 - 4

We can imagine the moment when Jacob asked the Lord for a blessing. He was desperate. He was *crying*. He was empty. He was in need.

Jacob wouldn't submit! He had to have his hip permanently injured to stop and look God in the eyes. God met him there, staring into Jacob's tear filled eyes and spoke to him.

> "What is your name?"
> Genesis 32:27b

Ummmm, hold up! We thought this man was God. Why did He ask Jacob for his name? Didn't He already know?

Rewind! Let's check out the meaning of Jacob's name.

+ Find Genesis 25:26. What does Jacob's name mean?

Jacob literally means "heel-grasper." His name in context implies that he was a trickster. He was always doomed to be grasping for things, never quite the first to succeed and always having to scheme his way to the top. So when God asked him to say his name, He was actually making Jacob face who he was. Jacob had to face reality.

> ### "'Jacob,' he answered."
> **Genesis 32:27c**

What about you? Has God gotten you alone, looked you in the eyes, and asked you to face it?

To face your doubts? Your concerns? Your questions?

Maybe you grew up in church, then you got to college and, for the first time, you met people who had different beliefs than you. Did you have that moment of panic?

Well, what do I believe?

Maybe in your heart of hearts, you sometimes wonder if God is even real.

Is God actually for me?

Maybe you lay awake at night wondering if you were ever really saved at all.

What will happen to me when I die?

HARD TRUTH TIME!

+ Have you ever had doubts in your faith? What were they? How do these doubts make you feel?

+ Be honest, how have these doubts affected your relationship with God?

Remember Jacob's situation? He was *so* stressed about meeting Esau. God had called him to go home and told him he would be blessed because of it, but Jacob wasn't sure if God would be true to his word.

Jacob thought that Esau was the enemy, but the real enemy was himself. God had to conquer him.[2]

The reality is, when we wrestle with God, winning can't be our end goal. That's just not how God works. God is the ultimate victor, never losing or wavering. So when we encounter hard things that we need to struggle through with the Lord, the act of "overcoming" looks different.

When we go head-to-head with God, we have to lose.

If everything was easy and clear, there would be no reason for faith. We were made for the struggle! In fact, God invites it! Because it's in the struggle where we get the chance to be face-to-face with God. In the struggle, we get to really know Him. And then we find our victory in submission to His will and His goodness.

Jacob learned that lesson as he was desperately holding on to this mysterious man, begging for a blessing. He really had overcome, but he had done it by giving in and acknowledging that he needed what only God could supply.

Jacob, trickster and heel-grasper, was at rock bottom in the dirt with God. Which evidently was exactly where God was planning to do His best work; redemption was coming.

+ Read Genesis 32:8. What name did God give to Jacob? Why?

161

Israel. Does that ring any bells? The great nation of Israel—God's chosen people who will take a front seat for the rest of the Bible—got their name from here, in the mud. Jacob struggled with God, and he overcame the struggle when he finally looked his Father in the eyes and asked for help.

Israel (formerly known as Jacob), fresh off his miraculous renaming, asked the man what His name was. The man's nonanswer was an answer in itself.

> **"But he replied, 'Why do you ask my name?' Then he blessed him there."**
> **Genesis 32:29b**

Israel had just looked God in the face. He had gotten personal with Him, begging for His help in the struggle.

He knew who that man was.

You're right. God could have told him outright. He could have pulled out the "I AM" moment He uses later with Moses (Exodus 3:14). He could have even just flat out said "I'm God, duh." Wouldn't that have made it easier for Israel? Couldn't some kind of confirmation have made Israel more sure of the supernatural quality of the encounter he had just had?

But God didn't confirm. He didn't clarify. He challenged Israel to rely on his faith.

Then He blessed him.

How many times have you begged God for a sign?

God, if You're real, make it obvious! Show Yourself to me so I can be sure!

How many times have you been met with silence?

What if that silence, that lack of confirmation, is actually a blessing? God's silence could be an invitation for deeper intimacy with Him. It could be a hand held out to you, wrestle ready. It could be the chance to strengthen your faith.

+ Fill in the blanks from Hebrews 11:1.

"Now _____ is _____ in what we hope for and _____ about what we do not see."

Where does your confidence in your faith come from? Is it from signs and wonders? Is it from solid clarity? Or is your faith the choice to hope, resting assured of the character of your God even when you can't see?

Israel had just had a radical encounter with God. Those things change you. Check out what he said as he stood up and brushed the dirt off of his jeans.

> "... I saw God face to face, and yet my life was spared."
> Genesis 32:30b

Israel didn't need God's expressed confirmation to know that He was there. He knew, in faith, that God had just met with him. He also knew that God, in His mercy, had allowed him to struggle and graciously allowed him to lose.

Remember, it is good to lose.

Just so you know, that "loser" Israel, left that wrestling match and chose to bravely face his brother, armed with a new trust in his God.

And Esau greeted him with a hug.

The Bible tells us that Jacob/Israel walked away from that God-encounter with a limp. Why is that significant? Let's think back to doubting Thomas.

Thomas needed to see to believe. Jesus showed up and held out his hands and allowed Thomas to touch Him. Thomas probably held onto that memory for the rest of his life. When doubts came up again, which they probably did, Thomas could remember what his Savior's hands felt like. He could rest in that memory of an encounter with God.

Scholars label this moment in Scripture as a "Christophany." Basically meaning that this was an instance where Jesus showed up on earth before His birth in Bethlehem. Genesis says that this was God, but He was also a man. God and man? Sounds like someone we know! So if Jesus, our Savior, was willing to show up for Jacob in his struggle, wouldn't He also be willing to show up for you in yours?

God gave Israel a memory, too. That limp was a tangible reminder of God's realness, closeness, and power.

So what does that mean for us?

We know that God meets us in our struggle and isn't scared of our doubts. But we also know that He challenges us to rely on our faith, choosing to believe even when we cant see.

Reread John 20:29b.

> "Because you have seen me, you have believed; blessed are those who have not seen and yet have believed."
> John 20:29b

Choosing faith even when we can't see is a mark of spiritual maturity, and it's absolutely necessary in the Christian life, because we will never have definitive proof of everything. But God, in His grace, sometimes still decides to show up and meet us face-to-face. Sometimes He leaves us reminders of His presence, little signposts for His goodness in our lives.

Jesus showed up for Thomas and held out His hands.

Jesus wrestled with Israel and allowed him to walk away with a limp.

God will show up for you in your struggle, too. Maybe He will give you a miraculous, impossible-to-miss sign, or maybe He will answer your questions with silence. But He *will* show up. Our God is always in the struggle.

When you are weighed down by doubts, questions, and spiritual insecurity, look for your limp. Think back on a time when God really did show up, a time when for a moment you saw Him clearly. And remember that, even when He is silent, He is just as close as He was in your miracle moment.

Choose faith, even when you are in the midst of an all-night wrestling match with your Creator. Who knows? He might just look you in the eyes and give you a new name.

THINK IT THROUGH . . .

WHAT STOOD OUT TO YOU?

WHAT CONVICTED YOU?

WHAT DO YOU FEEL CALLED TO SHARE?

CONVERSATION STARTERS

+ Have you ever had doubts about God? Describe them below.

_____
_____
_____
_____

+ God needed to get Jacob alone for their showdown. Are you making time to be alone with God? Why or why not?

_____
_____
_____
_____
_____
_____
_____

+ Think back on a time when God showed up for you. How can you hold on to that memory when doubts and questions come your way?

_____
_____
_____
_____
_____
_____
_____
_____
_____
_____

CHAPTER 8

GOD'S FAVOR DOESN'T MAKE SENSE

GENESIS

CHAPTERS 36-40

Welcome to week 8 of our study of Genesis! We're proud of you for making it this far! Since you've now read thirty-five chapters of Genesis, we know you understand us when we say that the people of Genesis were a hot mess. This book makes *Keeping Up with the Kardashians* seem tame. Our next victim, Joseph, is not an exception to the rule. If Abraham was Kris Jenner, Joseph is our Kim K. He really set the ball rolling for the rest of the Old Testament. Read through Genesis 36 - 40 to get a good understanding of where the story is going. Summaries are always available to you if you need them.

LET'S REVIEW!

36 In chapter 36 we are given the line of Esau, marking a transition in the Genesis narrative.

37 Israel's son Joseph was clearly the favorite (being the hot wife's son and all), causing some tension with his brothers. He told them about a dream he had where they all bowed down to him, and understandably, they got even more upset. They eventually got so mad that they sold him into Egyptian slavery and told their father that he had died.

38 The Joseph narrative stops for a chapter to focus on the tragic story of Tamar. Her husband died, and his family kept her with them but wouldn't allow her to have children to receive the status and security that came with them. Eventually, she disguised herself as a prostitute and tricked her father-in-law into sleeping with her. She became pregnant and was counted as the righteous one.

39 Back to Joseph, he served an Egyptian named Potiphar and found favor with him, thanks to the Lord's provision. He had authority over everything in Potiphar's house and was trusted to take care of things. But Potiphar's wife lusted after Joseph. When he declined her advances, she had him thrown in jail. But God was with Joseph even in jail. He rose in the ranks and was successful under the warden.

40 Pharaoh's chief cupbearer and chief baker were thrown in jail, where they both had distressing dreams. With God's power, Joseph interpreted the dreams for them. His interpretations were correct, and the chief cupbearer was let out of jail, while the chief baker was executed. Sadly, Joseph stayed in jail, because the cupbearer forgot to ask Pharaoh to free him.

NOTES

_____
_____
_____
_____
_____
_____
_____
_____
_____
_____
_____
_____
_____
_____
_____
_____
_____
_____
_____
_____
_____
_____
_____

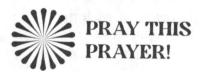

PRAY THIS PRAYER!

God, I know that You are in total control, and I love that I can rest in that knowledge. I'm sorry for every road block I set up for myself. Thank You for knocking all of them down. Please be with me this week as I learn what real favor looks like.

GOD'S FAVOR DOESN'T MAKE SENSE

GENESIS 37:1 - 36

It's easy to feel like we are walking a fine line when we are walking with the Lord. We tiptoe between "trusting" God's sovereignty *so* much that we feel like we have no say in our own lives and walking in the fear that we could mess everything up with one wrong move.

What does it really look like to be walking in the favor of the Lord? How do we know when we are on the right path?

+ Find John 15:5 and fill in the blanks below.

"I am the vine; you are the branches. If you _____ in me and I in you, you will _____ much _____ ; apart from me you can do _____ ."

When we are walking with the Lord, we bear fruit. So as a test to see if we are on the right track, we can look at our lives and see if we can find some godly fruit.

But what is godly fruit?

+ Find Galatians 5:22 - 23 and write down the fruits of the Spirit listed there.

Now look at your list. Do you notice what things are missing from it?

Success.

Popularity.

The approval of the people around you.

When we are walking with the Lord, lots of good things will grow in us and flow out of us. There is no denying that. But sometimes the good things of the world don't come *to* us. That means that we can't judge our heavenly success by our earthly success, and we can't judge God's approval by man's approval.

Joseph, the next in line in the Genesis narrative, had to learn that lesson the hard way. In fact, this guy's crazy life is the perfect example of having God's favor when it doesn't make earthly sense.

Are you ready? Let's dive in!

Read Genesis 37:1 - 2.

We have transitioned from Jacob (Israel) to Joseph. Now that we are this far into Genesis, we'd be surprised if you haven't noticed a certain pattern popping up. We've been hopping from dude to dude, following one family line.

The majority of the book of Genesis follows the "Patriarchs." If you were to take a course on Genesis, or even an Old Testament introduction class, the Patriarchs would be one of the very first concepts you'd learn about. Now, before we have a girl power meltdown, these Patriarchs aren't a symbol of male domination or an expression of modern day patriarchal values. It's simply a title to define a thread in the story. Genesis follows Abraham's family line, hopping from son to son.

This study, by nature of the book it covers, has also been following the patriarchal line.

+ Fill in the men we've learned about so far in the spaces below, starting with Abraham. Flip back in your book for help.

Abraham
Joseph

These sons are always like their fathers: a little bit messed up but covered by the grace of God. Joseph is no exception to this rule, as we will see in our study today.

In verse 2, we learn two things about Joseph.

1. He was seventeen at this point (probably also a dancing queen).
2. He was a snitch.

Okay, well maybe we can't assume that he was a snitch. Maybe he was just being honorable by bringing bad reports of his siblings to his father . . .

But it sounds pretty snitchy to us.

Joseph, like his ancestors before him, was not perfect and had some major flaws (what seventeen-year-old boy doesn't?). Those flaws caused him to make some big mistakes in this narrative. We already see the first one in verse 2.

Joseph used his favor to elevate himself.

Read Genesis 37:3 - 4 to see what we mean.

Joseph was on the receiving end of some toxic favoritism from his father Jacob. He had a softer job on the family farm and a higher status than all of his brothers. That could definitely be interpreted as favor, or undeserved preference from God! But if it was favor, Joseph did not handle it in the right way. He lorded his status over his brothers, taking every opportunity to remind his father that he was better than them.

And as we all know, snitches get stitches.

Verse 4 tells us that Joseph's eleven brothers hated him. In fact, they hated him so much—or were perhaps so jealous of him—that they, "could not speak a kind word to him." Before you go on feeling too sorry for Joseph, let's watch him dig his hole a little deeper.

Read Genesis 37:5 - 8.

So Joseph had this dream.

+ Summarize Joseph's first dream in the space below.

Nowadays we see dreams a little differently than they did in Joseph's time. We see our dreams as crazy things our brains cook up while we are sleeping, though they can occasionally have some meaning for us or perhaps even be from the Lord. In the Old Testament, a dream is *never* referred to as a simply human or psychological phenomenon. They are only referred to as moments of spiritual significance.[1]

So when the Bible says that Joseph had a dream, it means that Joseph received a message from the Lord while he was sleeping. If we think about it, that is pretty dang cool! But how did Joseph react to such an honor?

He got his second strike of this story.

Joseph used a God-given dream for his own pride.

The dream that God gave to Joseph was pretty easy to interpret: One day Joseph's brothers would bow down to him. Obviously the logical next step was *not* to go blabbing that dream to his brothers. Nobody wants to hear that they will someday have to bow to their annoying kid brother. But that's exactly what Joseph did. Yes, the dream was a good gift from the Lord, but by allowing his pride to make decisions for him, Joseph turned that good gift into a bad situation.

> "And they hated him all the more because of his dream and what he had said."
> Genesis 37:8b

Before we go any further, let's clarify something. This story is not supposed to be all about Joseph's messes. If you've come this far and are starting to get annoyed, because you thought you were going to figure out what it looks like to follow God's plan and so far it's all about Joseph being an idiot, don't panic. We're getting to that.

But it's still important to address Joseph's failings. Why? Because just as it was for Joseph, it's possible for us to be walking in the path of the Lord, benefiting from His favor, and still allow our sin to set up stumbling blocks for us along the way. We'll see Joseph's journey have crazy ups and downs, yet he still ended up where the Lord wanted him. But we wonder . . .

Did Joseph have to go through all the bad stuff to get to where God wanted him to be?

As we continue on, try not to read Joseph's messes as silly things that could have been avoided. We challenge you to see yourself in them.

The silver lining is that God still used Joseph anyway. He will do the same for you.

+ Have you seen a time in your life when sin made it harder to pursue God's best for your life? What was it like?

Joseph's brothers were mad. But apparently Joseph had a "haters gonna hate" kind of attitude, because he really took it a step too far with his next dream.

+ Read Genesis 37:9 - 11. Summarize Joseph's second dream in the space below.

Poor Joseph couldn't seem to take a hint. He had another dream from the Lord about ruling over his family, this time including his father and his mother Rachel (remember her?). He rushed to tell the whole family about it. As expected, they were not excited to hear this particular word from the Lord.

> **"His brothers were jealous of him, but his father kept the matter in mind."**
> **Genesis 37:11**

Strike three for Joseph.

He used his favor to hurt others.

For Joseph, the love, acceptance, and calling from God wasn't enough. He needed his family to see his calling, too. He was so desperate for their approval that he ignored all the signs of the pain that the message was causing them.

Yes, it was exciting news to hear from God. Favor was coming for Joseph! But in his rush to tell the whole world about it, perhaps even expecting them to bow down right then and there, he hurt those who were closest to him. He used God's word for an unholy purpose.

And there were consequences.

Read Genesis 37:12 - 17.

This little transition in the narrative may seem inconsequential. We know that Joseph was about to get the—possibly deserved—smackdown from his brothers. We read this part and feel tempted to skip it, because we want to get right to the drama. But pay attention here! We see that Joseph was sent out to find his brothers, but he didn't find them right away. In fact, he ran into a man.

+ Find Genesis 37:14 - 15. Where was Joseph when he ran into this mysterious man?

Shechem! In the Bible you can assume that every detail is significant to the story. Even the places we see characters go are important. Shechem was a place of promise. It's where God confirmed His promise to Abraham when he first arrived in Canaan (Genesis 12:6). And weirdly enough, it's actually where Joseph would eventually be buried (Joshua 24:32).

We don't think this was a random occurrence. God made Joseph stop on his way to one of the hardest moments of his life. Stopping was his reminder of God's promise, whether he realized it or not. Joseph didn't know that he was about to be taken into Egypt and would undergo many trials. But God's promise to give this land to Abraham's descendants would not be stopped. Joseph would return.

+ How does it make you feel to know that God's promises don't change even when our circumstances do?

Then, little Joe found his brothers. This was not a heartwarming family reunion.

+ Fill in the blanks from Genesis 37:18.

"But they saw him in the distance, and before he reached them, they _____ to _____ him."

That's intense! We have all been jealous of people who get more opportunities than us, and we have all been annoyed by people who constantly employ the "humble brag." But none of us go on and MURDER them for it.

Remember what we learned about dreams in the Old Testament? They are *always* from the Lord. Whether or not they liked it, Joseph's brothers must have known that this message was from God. So not only were they plotting to kill their baby bro, but they were also attempting to stop God's plan. They wanted to see if they could defeat God's Word.[2]

Seems like Joseph wasn't the only one with a pride problem.

Go ahead and skim through the rest of the story (verses 19 - 36).

A lot went down there, and we could honestly spend a whole semester breaking it down. Let's just hit the highlights.

The brothers initially wanted to kill Joseph, but they settled on just selling him instead. Why not make some money off of him? When he rolled up to the crew, they stripped him of his fancy robe (a symbol of his favor from his father and the Lord) and threw him into an empty cistern.

Check out this detail!

> **"The cistern was empty; there was no water in it."**
> **Genesis 37:24b**

Now check out what Jesus said in John 4:14.

> **"... but whoever drinks the water I give them will never thirst. Indeed, the water I give them will become in them a spring of water welling up to eternal life."**
> **John 4:14**

Water is life. For Joseph, the empty cistern symbolized barrenness, no hope for life.

Luckily, Jesus is a well that never runs dry. God's hand was still on Joseph's life, even in the dryest wasteland.

Joseph was sold into slavery to some merchants that came by the cistern. His brothers covered up their crime by convincing their father that Jacob was dead, mauled by a wild animal.

GOSPEL LENS

Our Savior Jesus gives us the water of eternal life. His salvation is a well that never runs dry. Are you feeling so tired and worn out in your faith? Is your time in the Word starting to feel dry? Remember that Jesus, who died on the cross and rose again for your victory, offers you living water. Stop living in the desert when Jesus opened up the floodgates.

> "Then Jacob tore his clothes, put on sackcloth and mourned for his son many days. All his sons and daughters came to comfort him, but he refused to be comforted. 'No,' he said, 'I will continue to mourn until I join my son in the grave.' So his father wept for him."
> Genesis 37:34 - 35

Notice how their father wasn't called Israel here. Jacob, our classic deceiver, got deceived by his own sons. This family had some major issues.

The chapter ends when Joseph was brought to Egypt and sold to Potiphar, one of Pharaoh's officials. We will continue to follow Joseph's story in the weeks to come, but let's take a moment to look for the character of God in this whole mess.

The story started with Joseph's dream from the Lord. God was the instigator here; He made His will for Joseph known. He told His chosen instrument that He was going to use him. Looking at the dreams, it really was good news for Joseph! But when Joseph went around sharing this dream with others, things started to go downhill. I mean, the guy was sold into slavery ultimately because of this dream God had given him.

So how can we say that Joseph was favored by the Lord?

+ Let's look ahead. Find these verses in your Bible:

Genesis 39:2

Genesis 39:20 - 21

Genesis 41:52

+ What theme do you see emerge in these verses?

The Lord was with Joseph wherever he was, even when he was at rock-bottom.

According to how we see God's hand in Joseph's life, the favor of the Lord does not equal the favor of the world. God's favor works in spite of and in the middle of the worst things the world has to offer.

Think about your own life. Are you at rock-bottom? Or have you ever been so down on your luck that you thought the Lord must be punishing you? Have you ever been tempted to judge your standing with God by your circumstances?

Maybe you are in the pit of depression, and you wonder if the Lord has abandoned you.

Maybe your family life is so bad that you think the Lord has forgotten about you.

Maybe you stepped out in faith, trusting that the Lord would provide, only to fail.

HARD TRUTH TIME!

+ **Think of a time when you were unsuccessful in the eyes of the world. How did that affect your view of God?**

+ **Now think of that earthly failure and look for the fruits of the Spirit you listed earlier. Was there something the Lord was growing in you during your time in the cistern?**

How do we answer our earlier question? Was Joseph's pride getting in the way of God's plan?

Yes *and* No.

Yes, Joseph was wrong to use God's good message for selfish ends. He wanted to rush things. He wanted recognition immediately and didn't care who he stepped on in the process.

But Joseph was not big enough to get in the way of God's plan.

We hate to break it to you, but *you are not big enough to get in the way of God's plan either.*

Sure, we are sinners, and we tend to set up walls that God didn't build. We create our own roadblocks and complain when we have to go around them. But our God is bigger and mightier than any power your sins, failures, and mess ups could ever have.

You can't get in His way.

God knew who Joseph was when He called him! He gave a big dream to a guy whose full time job was snitching on his brothers and spot-treating his fancy robe. Even when Joseph was running around acting the fool, God still had His hand on him. Even when Joseph was reaping the consequences of his actions, God was using him for good.

God's crazy, impossible-to-understand favor is on you, too. No matter where you are.

+ **Fill in the blanks from Proverbs 3:5 - 6 below.**

" _____ in the LORD with all your heart and lean not on your own _____ ; in all your ways _____ to him, and he will make your paths _____ ."

Stop relying on your own understanding! Just because your life isn't the essence of "worldly success," doesn't mean that your God doesn't love you, doesn't have a good plan for you, or isn't for you!

Walking in the will of God does not equal the favor of man!

If you are a child of God who has submitted your life to Him, His favor is on you whether you can see it or not. Try letting Him guide you. Try giving up control.

He really does love you. He really is for you. It's time to believe it.

THINK IT THROUGH . . .

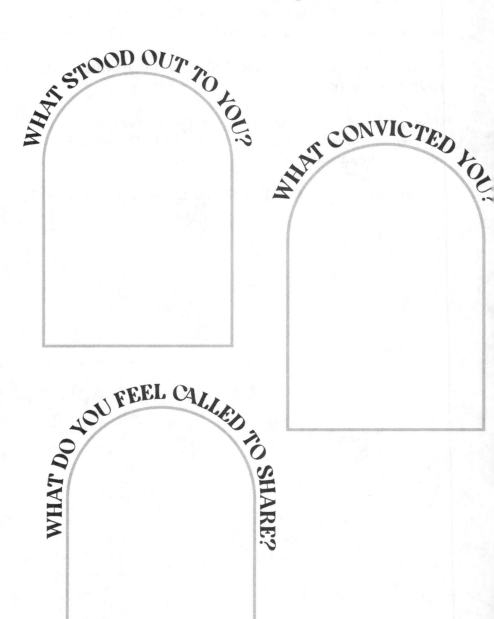

WHAT STOOD OUT TO YOU?

WHAT CONVICTED YOU?

WHAT DO YOU FEEL CALLED TO SHARE?

CONVERSATION STARTERS

+ Think of a time when you were at rock-bottom by earthly standards. Were you tempted to feel abandoned by God? Why?

_____

_____

_____

_____

+ Joseph was setting up his own roadblocks. In your own life, where might you be doing the same?

_____

_____

_____

_____

_____

_____

+ Sometimes it's hard to see God's favor. Think about your current situation. Where can you find His hidden blessings?

_____

_____

_____

_____

_____

_____

_____

_____

CHAPTER 9

GOD BRINGS US TOGETHER

GENESIS

CHAPTERS 41-45

Welcome to the second to last week of our Genesis study! How in the world has it gone by so fast? This week we get to continue on with Joseph's story. You may need to chug an energy drink real quick, because our teaching this week covers FOUR WHOLE CHAPTERS! We do things all out here at Delight, and we don't want to miss a second of the beautiful redemption story that God had in store for Joseph and his family. So don't worry! We will walk you through it step by step. For now, start by reading through Genesis 41 - 45 and check out the summaries for extra context.

LET'S REVIEW!

41 Years after Joseph's prophecy released the cupbearer from prison, Pharaoh had a dream that he couldn't understand. He asked all of his officials to interpret it, but no one could. The chief cupbearer remembered Joseph, and Pharaoh had him brought out of prison. Joseph, with God's power, interpreted Pharaoh's dream to mean that famine was coming to Egypt. Pharaoh believed him and put him in charge of all of Egypt, second only to Pharaoh himself. Joseph thrived in his position and had two sons. Under his guidance, Egypt was successful and well equipped, even when the famine came.

42 When the famine reached Jacob's family, he sent all of his sons (except Benjamin) to go to Egypt for food. They met with Joseph but didn't recognize him. Joseph played games with them, accusing them of being spies. He imprisoned Simeon and told them to come back with Benjamin.

43 Eventually, Jacob and his family ran out of grain. The brothers were forced to go back to Egypt, this time with Benjamin. Joseph, still unrecognized, welcomed them and fed them dinner.

44 As a final test, Joseph had his servants hide a silver cup in Benjamin's bag. When the brothers left, Joseph and his men chased them down and accused them of stealing. Joseph demanded that Benjamin be made a slave. The brothers were distressed and pleaded with Joseph for Benjamin's life.

45 Finally, Joseph came clean and revealed his identity to his brothers. They were afraid that he would still be mad at them, but Joseph, wiser from his years of suffering and growth, told them that it was all in God's plan. He welcomed his brothers with open arms. He told them to go get Jacob and come live in Egypt.

NOTES

_____
_____
_____
_____
_____
_____
_____
_____
_____
_____
_____
_____
_____
_____
_____
_____
_____
_____
_____
_____
_____
_____
_____
_____
_____

 **PRAY THIS PRAYER!**

God, You are the definition of grace. You forgive me when I don't deserve it, and You love me even when I'm far away. I'm sorry for not giving that same grace to the people around me. Thank You for Your conviction and Your invitation for a fresh start. Guide me in Your way. I want to look more like You.

GOD BRINGS US TOGETHER

GENESIS 42 - 45

Have you ever seen *The Princess Diaries*? (If you haven't, close your book right now and go watch it because it's amazing.)

It's widely acknowledged to be a *great* movie, no doubt because of the stellar cast (Julie Andrews *and* Anne Hathaway) and dreamy "from not to hot" storyline that was oh so popular in the early 2000s. It had us all fantasizing about being princesses, visiting Genovia, and getting makeovers from Paolo.

But have you noticed the unlikely and sometimes missed villain in the story? Princess Mia's best friend, Lilly.

When Mia found out that she was a princess, Lilly did *not* react well. She made fun of Mia and didn't really manage to stand by Mia's side when she needed her most. But in the end, they made up and Mia forgave her.

Their reconciliation leaves us with a weird sense of injustice. Lilly was *so* rude and selfish throughout the whole movie, and Mia just forgave her? Shouldn't Lilly have apologized more for her actions? Shouldn't there have been some consequences?

Forgiveness is hard. And it's especially hard when we have to forgive someone who doesn't deserve it. And on top of that, then we have to forget about it? It's even harder to do that.

+ Fill in the blanks from Ephesians 4:32.

"Be kind and compassionate to one another, _____ each other, just as in _____ God _____ you."

Our God is a God of forgiveness. Not only does He forgive us freely when we don't deserve it, but He also asks us to forgive others. It's a staple of the Christian life. In fact, the Bible says that people know we are Christians by how well we love others (John 13:35), and you have to learn how to forgive people if you want to love them well. Because as we will see in Joseph's story, sometimes people are jerks.

Forgiveness is necessary.

Let's recap. Think back to last week's story. We left off with poor, snitchy Joseph getting sold into slavery in Egypt. His jerky brothers convinced their father that he had died, and they went on with their lives. But God was with Joseph. After an undeserved stint in jail, he ended up in front of Pharaoh to interpret a dream through the power of God.

Check out Pharaoh's response when Joseph's interpretation was correct:

> "Then Pharaoh said to Joseph, 'Since God has made all this known to you, there is no one so discerning and wise as you. You shall be in charge of my palace, and all my people are to submit to your orders. Only with respect to the throne will I be greater than you.'"
> Genesis 41:39 - 40

Joseph had his own *Princess Diaries* moment! He went from teen slave, to prisoner, to second in command over all of Egypt.

But God wasn't finished yet.

+ Read Genesis 42:1 - 5 and summarize below.

[blank box]

Those five verses give us a pretty thorough setup. Jacob/Israel heard that there was grain in Egypt while his family had none, so he sent ten of his sons to go to Egypt to get some. He kept Benjamin home with him, because Benjamin was the last son left of his beloved wife Rachel. He couldn't stand to lose him like he lost Joseph.

Notice the brothers' reactions when Jacob proposed the plan . . .

> ## "Why do you just keep looking at each other?"
> Genesis 42:1b

It doesn't look like Joseph's brothers were too crazy about going to Egypt. Maybe their father's plan reminded them of the boy they had sent there to be enslaved. They had the decency to be a little wary. But more than wariness, this is the first moment where we get a glimpse of something important:

Joseph's brothers felt the guilt of their actions.

Despite their immediate concern, the brothers headed out to Egypt. God's plan for redemption was set in motion.

Why? Because division cannot stand in the family of God.

Read Genesis 42:8 - 9.

Uhhh . . . What?!

Let's rewind a little. So the bros travelled to Egypt and had to go
before Joseph to buy the much needed grain, because he was lord
of the land and all that. Joseph recognized them immediately, but
they didn't recognize him. Then Joe pulled out a strange move. He
acted like an angry stranger and accused his brothers of being spies.

This just went from *The Princess Diaries* to *A Series of Unfortunate
Events*. It doesn't make any sense! Why was Joseph playing games
with them? We need to address this now, because the game-playing
continues throughout the rest of the story.

There are different theories behind Joseph's odd behavior. You
are welcome to pick your favorite, or do what we do and choose a
"both and" perspective.

1. Joseph was really mad at his brothers and had an elaborate plan
   for revenge.
2. Joseph was torn between forgiving his brothers and making
   them pay for their actions.
3. God was using Joseph to bring the brothers to repentance.

Honestly, looking at the different interpretations, it makes sense
that it could be all three at once. Listen to how this scholar puts it:

*"And if we could ask God's opinion about what is going on, perhaps
God would reckon that the brothers do need to be brought to a deep
and genuine repentance, that the way Joseph is treating them does
have the capacity to bring this about, and that even if Joseph's
resentment is driving him more than it should—well, God works
through human weakness and sin as well as through human strength
and righteousness (as Joseph himself will eventually point out)."*[1]

Whatever the motivations, Joseph's weird actions here were a catalyst for the reunification and forgiveness this family needed. Thank you, Lord!

And here's another juicy little tidbit that really proves the Lord's direct involvement:

> **"So when Joseph's brothers arrived, they bowed down to him with their faces to the ground."**
> **Genesis 42:6b**

Remember Joseph's dreams from last week? This is *definitely* ringing a bell!

Joseph's brothers were starting to resemble those sheaves of grain (go back to Genesis 37:5 - 7 if you need a refresher).

Here is where Joseph, always wildin', accused them of being spies and threw them into jail. After three days, he let them out and ordered them to return with their youngest brother. We catch the brothers' response in verse 21:

> **They said to one another, 'Surely we are being punished because of our brother. We saw how distressed he was when he pleaded with us for his life, but we would not listen; that's why this distress has come on us.'"**
> **Genesis 42:21**

Again, they were reminded of their guilt. They blamed their bad fortune in Egypt on their mistreatment of Joseph. But that's no surprise! That is what unconfessed sin and withheld forgiveness does to us; it's poisonous.

+ Have you ever allowed a secret sin to fester in your heart? Do you have one now? What does it feel like?

- Feels like pent up tension / confusion
- Steals Happiness + creates worry

The brothers went home weighed down by guilt and by the extra silver that sneaky Joseph placed in their bags (remember, embrace the weird!). They had to leave their brother Simeon as collateral as they prepared to ask Jacob for Benjamin.

Read Genesis 42:38.

Jacob was not going to let Ben go. God had to intervene.

As we begin chapter 43, we see that the famine was still raging and Jacob's family had run out of food.

> "... their father said to them, 'Go back and buy us a little more food.'"
> Genesis 43:2b

We can imagine the deep breath the brothers must have taken, preparing to remind their father what going back to Egypt would mean. They knew it wouldn't be easy to convince Jacob to part with Benjamin.

Judah stepped up.

> **"I myself will guarantee his safety; you can hold me personally responsible for him. If I do not bring him back to you and set him here before you, I will bear the blame before you all my life."**
> **Genesis 43:9**

This intervention from Judah is significant. Think about it! He really knew what it was like to hold the weight of the blame. He had already taken one son away from his father. He was promising that he would not lose another.

So Jacob let them go, giving in with a feeling of defeat. The brothers loaded up with gifts for the mysterious Egyptian official (*cough* Joseph *cough*) and headed on their way.

Read Genesis 43:26 - 34.

The poor brothers were probably experiencing some major whiplash. They came to Joseph expecting anger and threats, but they were instead greeted with friendly questions and a fancy meal.

What about Joseph?

+ How do you think Joseph was feeling based on verses 26 - 34?

It seems like whatever rage had taken over Joseph during their last visit was gone. Suddenly, he was eager to hear about his father, to see his long lost brother, and to provide his family with a nice meal.

In fact, he was overcome with emotion.

From what we know about complicated family situations, we can totally relate to what Joseph was feeling. Sure they had hurt him, but they were his family. We can understand that! That bond—that love—runs deep.

Can you see the character of God here?

We are all His children, a part of His family. As our Father, the Lord can't help but to welcome us back with open arms, even when we've hurt Him. His love for us is so much bigger than our mistakes. And He is not content with being the only one who loves like that.

+ Fill in the blanks from 1 John 4:19.

"We _____ because he _____ loved us."

God has given us so much grace, so much forgiveness, and so many chances. We wonder what it would look like for us to do the same for the people around us, our family in Christ.

Now forget about the warm and fuzzies you're feeling. Things are about to get weird again.

Read Genesis 44:1 - 2.

Joseph was back at his games. This time, he orchestrated the meeting so that Benjamin would be accused of stealing. Let's see what went down.

+ Skim over the rest of chapter 44 and summarize what happened between Joseph and his brothers in the space on the next page.

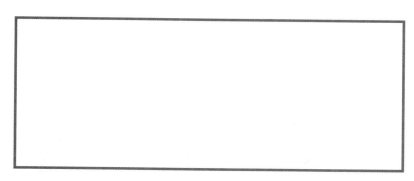

It was mostly divination, silver cups, and random accusations, but we want you to pay attention to what happened at the end. Judah was not going to let Benjamin become enslaved, especially for this made-up crime that Joseph accused him of. They were not going to leave without their brother.

> **"Now then, please let your servant remain here as my lord's slave in place of the boy, and let the boy return with his brothers. How can I go back to my father if the boy is not with me? No! Do not let me see the misery that would come on my father."**
> **Genesis 44:33 - 34**

This was the turning point. It was like God had planned out these events to almost mirror *exactly* what had happened to Joseph. They had to decide whether their youngest brother, clearly the new favorite of their father, was going to be enslaved for their comfort or if they were going to choose the hard thing and step out in love.

They chose correctly this time.

Read Genesis 45:1 - 2.

His brothers' clear change of heart moved Joseph. He couldn't play games with them anymore. We imagine him whipping off his wig and dramatically wiping off some kohl eyeliner. The brothers must have been SHOOK. There, right in front of them, was their long lost brother, weeping uncontrollably.

Verse 3 confirms how shook the bros were.

> "... they were terrified at his presence."
> Genesis 45:3b

Their demons had literally surfaced right in front of them. For years they had mourned their actions and felt the guilt of, in effect, killing their own brother. They had to watch their father's depression as he dealt with the loss of his favorite son. They had kept a secret that tore their insides apart.

Then suddenly, there he was, standing right in front of them. Brother Joe was dressed as an Egyptian official, and he had total power over their life. He could choose to feed them or leave them to starve.

What would you do if you were in Joseph's shoes?

Think of the people who have wronged you. Think about that boy that took advantage of you. Think of that friend that betrayed you. Think of that estranged family member that you know you can never forgive.

What if you were suddenly standing over them while they bowed down at your feet. With one wave of your hand, you could force them to deal with the consequences of their actions.

Or you could forgive.

HARD TRUTH TIME!

+ Is there someone you haven't forgiven? Who? Why?

> I think I am pretty forgiving, but I have situations w/ built up resentment.

+ Be honest, do you want to forgive them? Why or why not?

> Yes, but I say that on the surface — deep work needs to be done.

Forgiveness, especially when the other person has done nothing to earn it, feels like peeling off a layer of our own skin. Our need for justice and our desire for retribution hold us back. We want them to hurt the way that they hurt us. We want them to understand that what they did was wrong. We want them to know that they are unforgivable.

But what if God asked you to forgive them?

What if He brought them to you—right at your feet—and gave you a choice?

We know what we should choose.

But it would be so tempting to choose wrong.

Luckily, God gave us this story about Joseph and his brothers. Let's see what Joseph chose.

Read Genesis 45:4 - 8.

+ **Fill in the blanks from Genesis 45:8a.**

"So then, it was _____ _____ who sent me here, but ____ ."

Wow. Do you have goosebumps? Joseph didn't just forgive, though his speech was moving and powerful. He actually absolved them of any blame. He wiped their slates clean, saying that it was God's plan all along. He held nothing against them.

That sounds a lot like what God does for us!

+ **Copy Psalm 103:12 in the space below.**

God has *removed our transgressions*. He isn't up there holding on to every little bad thing we have ever done, counting them against us! When we come to him and confess, He actually *forgets* our sins! He looks at us and sees us as clean, because He has given us His own righteousness.

So when Joseph looked at his brothers through God's eyes, he saw the whole picture. He saw God's plan and the lives that had been saved. He saw the fulfillment of the dream the Lord had given him, and he saw his brothers' worth, despite their flaws. He forgave them fully, without any bitterness, and forgetting all transgressions.

Jesus Christ died on the cross for the forgiveness of your sins. While you were still sinning, He decided you were worth it. He decided you were worth forgiving. When He looks at you, He sees a beloved child. You can come to Him with anything. There is power in confession, and your Savior is *always* ready to forgive.

How in the world are we supposed to do that?

The answer may feel cliche, a little bit too "Hobby Lobby" or "Live Laugh Love," but that doesn't make it any less true.

We need to let go and let God.

The Bible says that when we are in Christ, we are a new creation. The old is gone, and the new has come (2 Corinthians 5:17). That means that we have the same power that raised Jesus from the dead living inside of us! We have the same power that fed the five thousand, healed lepers, and turned water into wine.

We even have the same power that helped Joseph forgive his brothers all those years ago.

So then, the trick is to allow the Holy Spirit to use you. Choose to let go of yourself: your pain, your pride, even your own sense of justice. Choose to let God work through you. The cool thing is you actually give the Spirit more room to work through that surrender! And He is working for the good of those who love Him!

+ Fill in the blanks from Romans 8:28.

"And we know that in _____ things God works for the _____ of those who _____ him, who have been called according to his purpose."

We know that God is capable of carrying out justice (think back to week 2!). Joseph knew the same. By forgiving his brothers, by welcoming them back into his arms, by providing for them, he put back into God's hands what belonged there the whole time.

God will take care of the details.

So think about your life. Think about the unforgiveness you are holding on to. Is it hurting you? Is it poisonous?

Is it time to let it go?

Remember, disunity cannot stand when you are a child of God. He will *always* bring His children back together. Open your hands and forgive. God can handle the rest.

THINK IT THROUGH . . .

WHAT STOOD OUT TO YOU?

WHAT CONVICTED YOU?

WHAT DO YOU FEEL CALLED TO SHARE?

CONVERSATION STARTERS

+ Who do you need to forgive? Why? Spill allllll the details here.

An ex: built up resentment, I didn't deserve what happened.

Myself - W/ PTSD related stuff

+ Have you ever fully accepted God's forgiveness for yourself? What unconfessed sin do you need to bring to Him?

Sometimes it is hard + other times I take it for granted

Sexual sin / not praising him more in front of others,

+ Joseph wiped his brothers' slates clean with the help of the power of God. What would it look like for you to do the same for those who have wronged you?

Good, but its easy to have that view in my eyes, but what about theirs

CHAPTER 10

GOD ISN'T FINISHED YET

GENESIS

CHAPTERS 46-50

Well it looks like you have another thing to add to your resume: Genesis expert. You have successfully made it through *the whole book*! You deserve a little pat on the back! But even more important than knowing every detail of the first book of the Bible, over the past ten weeks you have become more acquainted with God, your Creator. You have taken time to sit in His presence, to hear His voice, and to learn more of His heart. That's pretty cool.

This week we are going to wrap things up by *not* wrapping things up. In your reading, you'll notice that Genesis doesn't end in a beautiful, heartwarming conclusion. Why? Because Genesis is just the beginning. Don't let that get you down though. Let it excite you! There is always more to learn. Go ahead and read Genesis 46 - 50 and take some notes, using our nifty chapter summaries as needed.

LET'S REVIEW!

46 Jacob/Israel was overjoyed to find out that his favorite son was alive. The family packed up and moved to Egypt under Joseph's guidance.

47 Because Pharaoh was so pleased with Joseph, he allowed Jacob/Israel's family to settle in the land of Goshen and continue their herding. Jacob blessed Pharaoh, and Joseph continued to bring prosperity upon Egypt and Pharaoh's house. Jacob was getting old though, and he made Joseph swear to bury him back home.

48 Before Jacob/Israel died, Joseph brought his sons to him to be blessed. Sticking to the tradition, Jacob blessed the younger son over the older, which we're finding is on brand for God's upside down Kingdom.

49 Chapter 49 of Genesis gives us Jacob/Israel's last words: a blessing to each of his twelve sons. Remember these twelve sons became the twelve tribes of Israel. As he took his final breath, Jacob asked to be buried with his ancestors.

50 Joseph and his family mourned Jacob/Israel and buried him where he had asked. Because their father had died, Joseph's brothers worried that he would turn on them. Joseph reassured them that God used their evil for good. He lived 110 years, and when he died, he asked to be brought out of Egypt with his people when the time came.

NOTES

_____
_____
_____
_____
_____
_____
_____
_____
_____
_____
_____
_____
_____
_____
_____
_____
_____
_____
_____
_____
_____
_____
_____

 **PRAY THIS
PRAYER!**

God, I am so glad that You are in charge. Your goodness and power
are impossible to stop, and I'm so thankful for Your glorious love
that invades every aspect of my life. I'm sorry for losing sight of You
when things seem hopeless. Thank You for giving me firm pieces
of Yourself to hold on to when I feel like letting go. Please show me
where You are, even when I feel lost.

GOD ISN'T FINISHED YET

GENESIS 46:1 - 7; 50:22 - 26

There are two types of people in this world: the ones who love a good cliffhanger and the ones who don't. We would venture to say that most of us are in the "don't" camp. There is nothing more frustrating than getting to the end of a stressful movie or book, only to be left with no resolution, just a hanging clue that more of the story is coming.

The Marvel cinematic universe is great at this. They brought the "after credits" scene into fashion. True fans know to stay seated in that theater chair, because a big hint at the next movie comes after the boring list of names.

Although we still have to wait two years until they release the next installment, and by then all of the details have become fuzzy, so we have to rewatch the last movie.

Genesis is like a Marvel movie. Only instead of waiting two years for the resolution, the Israelites waited over 400 years.

But before we get too far ahead of ourselves, let's jump back into the story.

Last week we saw the beautiful reunion of Joseph and his brothers. It was cute. We shed some tears. After the hugs, the boys headed back to Canaan to tell their father the good news that Joseph was alive and to bring him into Egypt to escape the famine.

Read Genesis 45:25 - 28.

As could be expected, Jacob/Israel was pretty doubtful at first. It was incredible to imagine that his lost son could be a ruler in Egypt, a foreign powerhouse. But he was eventually persuaded and agreed to make the trip.

Now think about this trip. Jacob, a *really* old man at this point, was leaving behind the land that *God* had led him to and was heading to a foreign land that didn't even acknowledge his God. Admittedly, Jacob was used to being an alien in foreign lands, but still . . . this move to Egypt must have felt like a lot.

> "So Israel set out with all that was his, and when he reached Beersheba, he offered sacrifices to the God of his father Isaac."
> Genesis 46:1

Verse 1 seems like a transitional statement, but we think it's packed with significance.

+ What's the first thing you notice about Genesis 46:1?

Suddenly Jacob is back to being referred to as Israel.

+ Flip back to week 7. What is the significance of Jacob's second name, Israel?

Israel, he who struggles with God.

Perhaps the author calls him Israel at this moment because he was struggling with the idea of moving to Egypt. Or maybe he is called Israel here as a reminder of God's promise, even while on a detour.

Or both.

On top of that, the place that Jacob decided to stop and offer sacrifices to the Lord is also significant.

+ What's the place Israel stopped at in Genesis 46:1?

```


```

Beersheba! Remember, every detail has meaning. So let's do a little research.

+ Find Genesis 22:19. Who lived in Beersheba?

```


```

+ Now flip to Genesis 26:23. Search the surrounding verses to find out who else made a stop at Beersheba.

```


```

Beersheba was a place where Jacob's father Isaac had built an altar to the Lord. It was also the place his grandfather Abraham had stayed. It was a place of promise. And as we continue to read we'll see that Jacob needed a reminder of the promise before he jumped into the unknown.

Read Genesis 46:2 - 4.

Here we see a call. It's a classic example of God reaching out to a willing listener.

"Jacob! Jacob!"

"Here I am."

Just like his ancestors before him, Jacob was open and ready to listen to God's voice. He was called by name. He knew that God would figure out all the details. He just needed to be there. He needed to be available.

+ Think about your life. Have you made yourself available to the call of the Lord? Why or why not?

God grabbed Jacob's attention and told him to not be afraid, which happens to be a big spoiler that he must have been very afraid.

It's okay, Jacob, we can relate.

Are you scared right now? Are you worried that you will never know your purpose? Do you fear that what God is asking you to do is impossible? Or do you lie awake at night wondering if where you are now is where you are always going to be?

"Do not be afraid . . ."
Genesis 46:3b

Jacob felt that age old fear of the future and the unknown, and God responded with two important reminders that He still gives us today:

1. Who He is.
2. What He promises.

"I am God, the God of your father."
Genesis 46:3a

By now in our study, we are getting pretty familiar with the character of God. We know that He is good and that everything He does is good. Jacob must have known the character of God, too. He had heard the stories of God's goodness to his ancestors, and he had seen firsthand God's work in his own life and in the lives of his family. So when God reminded Jacob of who He was, he must have started to stand a little straighter.

In verse 4 God reminded Jacob of His promises, the covenant He had made with his family. God reminded him of the great nation that was coming and even told him that his beloved son would be with him when he died. But this is our favorite part of God's response:

"I will go down to Egypt with you, and I will surely bring you back again."
Genesis 46:4a

Does that remind you of another verse?

+ Find Matthew 28:20 and copy the second part of the verse in the space below.

```



```

Our God, who we know to be unfailingly good, promises to be with us *always*. Just like He promised Jacob all those years ago. Even when we are going into our own "Egypts"—our foreign lands that feel impossible to conquer—our good God promises to stand by our side.

What do we have to be afraid of?

Read Genesis 46:5 - 7.

Jacob must have felt like God's Word was good enough, because he set off obediently. He brought everything with him, trusting wholeheartedly in God's commands.

So Jacob got to Egypt, reunited with his long lost son, was granted a nice plot of land from Pharaoh, and settled down. We can imagine little bunnies hopping around, smiles on everyone's faces as a double rainbow paints the sky. A happy ending was imminent, right? Because it was *God* who told him to go there!

. . . Right?

+ Read Genesis 49:33. What was the ending actually like?

Jacob died. This man—who had followed God all of his life and was promised offspring and a great nation in a land that God had promised—died in a foreign desert surrounded by his, only recently, reunited sons. The next couple verses even tell us he was *embalmed* in the Egyptian style! What a burial for a Canaanite wanderer!

If you've been reading closely, this may seem kind of sad. It's anticlimactic. We're left with the feeling that more was supposed to happen. Even though he was old, did he live a full life? Was he sad to have died so far away from his homeland? What about the big stuff he was going to do for God? What about the promise?

Let's skip to the very end of Genesis to try to scratch that resolution itch. Maybe Joseph took up the mantle and made the big moves for the Kingdom.

Read Genesis 50:22 - 26.

Ummm . . . that's kind of a bummer! We thought this Egypt thing was temporary! Didn't God say He would bring them out of there?

It looks like Joseph, just like his father, was still holding on to God's Word.

+ Fill in the blanks from Genesis 50:24b.

"God will _____ come to your aid and take you up ____ of this _____ to the land he _____ on oath to Abraham, Isaac and Jacob."

Reading that verse can make a girl pretty incredulous. It's almost funny! How can they keep believing that God would come through on His promise when He told the same thing to four dudes across four generations who all died without seeing it fulfilled? We can just end this study now, because we've obviously learned a new characteristic of God!

God is SLOW!

Well, as much as you would love to slam your book closed right now, we have to let you in on a little secret.

God isn't actually as slow as He sounds.

Don't believe us? Check out this verse from 2 Peter:

"The Lord is not slow in keeping his promise, as some understand slowness. Instead he is patient with you, not wanting anyone to perish, but everyone to come to repentance."
2 Peter 3:9

If there was ever a moment where you were tempted to disagree with the Bible, this might be it. Let's press in.

How is God *not* slow? How could He have allowed Abraham, Isaac, Jacob, *and* Joseph to all die without seeing His promise to them fulfilled?

The easy way out here would be to use the "time is different for God" excuse. The Bible *does* say that a thousand years are like a day to the Lord (2 Peter 3:8), so maybe He just thought that His timing wouldn't bother anyone.

Unfortunately, there is a bit of an issue with that. God isn't oblivious. He isn't apathetic to our waiting. Don't you think He would notice if a bunch of people were thinking that He was taking too long? Doesn't He know what a year feels like in human time?

That means that God *knew* He was taking a long time. He knew that people were going to die while they waited on Him. He knew that (thousands of years in the future) some college women would read the ending of Genesis and question His ability to come through on time.

So why did He wait?

+ Check back on 2 Peter 3:9. If God isn't slow, then what is He?

```

```

Our God is patient. While we are waiting on God, He is waiting *for* us.

Let's use Joseph as an example. As we've learned, God gave Joseph a dream that his family would bow to him. Then, after probably thinking his life was going to be easy and filled with lavish good luck, he was enslaved and imprisoned for many years before finally getting to a place where he was standing over his groveling brothers.

Why did God let him serve as a slave? Why did God let him sit in that prison cell for so long? Doesn't that make Him slow to fulfill His promise?

Joseph didn't think so! Check out what he told his brothers as they feared retribution.

+ Fill in the blanks from Genesis 50:20.

"You intended to harm me, but _____ intended it for _____ to accomplish what is now being done, the saving of many lives."

There's that word again! *Good*. Joseph somehow was able to look back on his life and see the good that the Lord intended. He looked at his situation and chose to see God's immovable character first, refusing to define his God by his circumstances.

So when is slowness good?

When slowness is *patience*.

According to Joseph, God waited to fulfill His promise because there was an opportunity for lives to be saved. Think about it! Our God loves the world, as we learned in week 2. He could not have enjoyed the idea of allowing Joseph to sit in jail or endure trials! He *loved* Joseph even more than Jacob did! So what could make a God so in love with His children allow those same beloved children to suffer?

The knowledge of the salvation to come.

The book of Hebrews says, "For the joy set before him [Jesus] endured the cross, scorning its shame, and sat down at the right hand of the throne of God. Consider him who endured such opposition from sinners, so that you will not grow weary and lose heart" (Hebrews 12:2b - 3). Jesus was patient for us. He waited as we rebelled, as we fought, and even as we nailed Him to a cross. He had Kingdom vision for us; He decided that our salvation was worth the wait *and* worth the cross.

Through the diligent waiting of one beloved child, many lives would be saved. God saw the big picture and, at the end of his life, Joseph could see it, too.

What about Jacob? Remember what God had promised him?

> **"I will give you and your descendants the land on which you are lying ... I am with you and will watch over you wherever you go, and I will bring you back to this land. I will not leave you until I have done what I have promised you."**
> **Genesis 28:13b, 15**

For Jacob, God waited until after he had died to fulfill His promise. His bones were returned to the Promised Land to lay with Abraham and Isaac.

But what about those descendants? The ones who were now stuck in Egypt?

Let's check the after credit scene.

Read Exodus 3:9 - 10.

God called a guy named Moses to deliver the Israelite people from Egypt. But by then, over 400 years had gone by and the people were enslaved.

You're probably wondering how that could be patience.

Check those verses again. Do you notice anything?

"... the Israelite people ..."

In 400 years, under the oppression of Egypt, Jacob's family had grown into a people. A *nation*. They were exactly the kind of nation who could settle a land. Maybe even the land that God had promised. So through His patience, God allowed the children He loved to remain in, to endure, a trial. But He saw the end goal. He knew He was going to bring them out! He was determined to wait until every possible beloved one could be saved.

> "... not wanting anyone to perish, but everyone to come to repentance."
> 2 Peter 3:9b

The redemption story of when God brought His people out of Egypt is legendary. We're guessing that it was important enough to wait for.

So what about you?

Has God been slow to bring you a husband while you watch all of your friends getting their "ring by spring"?

Has God been slow in pointing you to your purpose? Is He just watching as you wander aimlessly through life, not really sure of a direction to follow?

Has God been slow in following through on a promise to you? Did you think you would be somewhere else by now?

Or could He actually be *patient*? Could your waiting be for your benefit and for the good of the ones He loves?

God is patiently maturing you, teaching you to love Him first whether in marriage or singleness.

God is patiently waiting for your purpose to unfold as He

orchestrates your life to light a passion in your heart. He's so excited about what He has in store, but He knows it's worth the incubation period.

God is patiently waiting to fulfill His promise to you. He watches you grow stronger in the trials, proud of you as He molds you into the incredible woman He made you to be.

+ **Be honest, do you see God's character clearly in the waiting?**

IF I DON'T SEE HIM, HE ISN'T THERE.	I'M NOT SURE IF I BELIEVE THAT HE IS FOR ME.	MAYBE HE LOVES ME, BUT HE HAS GIVEN UP ON USING ME.	I SEE HIM MOLDING ME AS I WAIT ON HIM.	I WAIT WITH JOY! I KNOW HE WILL ALWAYS COME THROUGH.

+ **In which area of your life has God been slow? What would it look like for you to believe in His patience?**

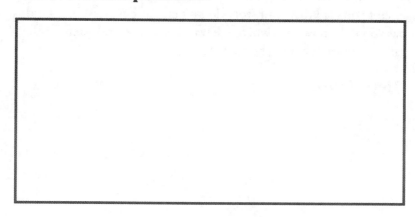

Why is it important to know the character of our God? Why do we need to become acquainted with His heart?

Because life is hard. It's scary. It's confusing. And sometimes it's downright terrifying.

Our human nature, the sinful flesh we are all born with, wants us to be cynical. It wants us to be hopeless. It wants us to look at our world and see only evidence of lack. It wants us to stop looking for God. But God isn't done looking for us. He is determined to chase us down, to prove His goodness to our clouded minds. He paints every sunset for you, so that you can look up and see His hand, His beauty.

You need to know who God is, because you were created *by* Him. You were created *for* Him. You were created to walk in communion *with* Him. Armed with the belt of truth and the shield of faith (Ephesians 6:14, 16), you can look at the world through a Jesus lens. You can look at your circumstances through a Jesus lens. You can even look at your trials through a Jesus lens.

Even in the waiting, when things are hard and the outlook seems bleak, you can squeeze the hand of the good Father who is walking by your side, knowing that He is always true to who He says He is.

As we wrap up our study of Genesis, you can be thankful for a cliffhanger God. Aren't you so grateful that He isn't done yet? Aren't you glad that your story doesn't end in Egypt? Where God has you right now isn't where He wants you forever. Listen for the call, and when it comes, be ready to say,

"Here I am."

THINK IT THROUGH . . .

WHAT STOOD OUT TO YOU?

WHAT CONVICTED YOU?

WHAT DO YOU FEEL CALLED TO SHARE?

CONVERSATION STARTERS

+ In what area of your life do you feel like God is being slow? Why?

_____

_____

_____

_____

+ It's hard to trust that God will come through on His word when we can't see the ending. What promises has He made to you? Do you trust Him to follow through?

_____

_____

_____

_____

_____

_____

+ We've spent the last ten weeks learning about God's character. Which of His characteristics do you need to claim over your situation today?

_____

_____

_____

_____

_____

_____

ABOUT THE AUTHOR

Hey! I'm Maggie!

I am working my DREAM JOB as Curriculum Development Coordinator here at Delight Ministries. I like to think of myself as Delight's translator! My job is to take God's powerful, perfect, and active Word and present it to college women in a way that helps them see how relevant and real it is for their own lives . . .
AND I LOVE IT!

In my free time, catch me eating a bowl of popcorn, reading a book, or hanging out with my hottie husband. I'm a die-hard Swiftie and I'm always down for a *Twilight* marathon. I'm an outfit repeater to the core, and my favorite song is "Chacarron" by El Chombo.

NOTES

01 | WEEK 1: GOD BREATHES LIFE

1. Dr. Tim Mackie, *Adam to Noah*, Classroom Beta by BibleProject, 17:30, https://bibleproject.com/blog/why-did-god-ask-abraham-to-sacrifice-isaac/.
2. David Guzik, *Genesis*, Enduring Word Commentary Series, (Goleta: Enduring Word Media, 2018).
3. Rich Mullins, "Awesome God," *Winds of Heaven, Stuff of Earth*, produced by Reed Arvin (Reunion: 1988).

02 | WEEK 2: GOD IS GOOD WHEN THINGS ARE BAD

1. John Goldingay, *Genesis for Everyone, Part 1: Chapters 1-16*, The Old Testament for Everyone, (Louisville, Westminster John Knox Press: 2010).
2. Dr. Walter Harrelson, *The New Interpreter's Study Bible*, (Nashville, Abingdon Press: 2003).
3. Goldingay, *Genesis for Everyone*.

03 | WEEK 3: GOD KEEPS YOU SAFE BUT CALLS YOU TO SCARY

1. "Abram's Journey to Canaan," https://www.nicepng.com/ourpic/u2t4t4u2t4y3u2y3_abrams-journey-to-canaan-abrahams-journey-from-ur/.
2. Whitney Woollard, "Covenants: The Backbone of the Bible," *BibleProject* (blog), 2018, https://bibleproject.com/blog/covenants-the-backbone-bible/?utm_source=web_social_share&medium=shared_blog.
3. David Guzik, *Genesis*, Enduring Word Commentary Series, (Goleta: Enduring Word Media, 2018).
4. Maverick City Music, "Jireh," *Old Church Basement*, produced by Chris Brown, Tony Brown, Steven Furtick, Jason Ingram, and Jonathan Jay, (Elevation Worship: 2021).

04 | WEEK 4: GOD WILL DRAG YOU OUT

1. David Guzik, *Genesis*, Enduring Word Commentary Series, (Goleta: Enduring Word Media, 2018).
2. Cory Asbury, "Reckless Love," *Reckless Love*, produced by Jason Ingram and Paul Mabury, (Bethel Music: 2017).

05 | WEEK 5: GOD IS WORTH YOUR SACRIFICE

1. David Guzik, *Genesis*, Enduring Word Commentary Series, (Goleta: Enduring Word Media, 2018).
2. Andy Patton, "Why Did God Ask Abraham to Sacrifice Isaac?" *BibleProject* (blog), 2020, https://bibleproject.com/blog/why-did-god-ask-abraham-to-sacrifice-isaac.
3. Guzik, *Genesis*.
4. Patton, "Why Did God?"

06 | WEEK 6: GOD SEES YOU

1. David Guzik, *Genesis*, Enduring Word Commentary Series, (Goleta: Enduring Word Media, 2018).
2. Peter Enns and Jared Byas, *Genesis for Normal People: A Guide to the Most Controversial, Misunderstood, and Abused Book of the Bible*, The Bible for Normal People Book Series, 2nd ed. (The Bible for Normal People, 2019).
3. Guzik, *Genesis*.

07 | WEEK 7: GOD IS IN THE STRUGGLE

1. David Guzik, *Genesis*, Enduring Word Commentary Series, (Goleta: Enduring Word Media, 2018).
2. Guzik, *Genesis*.

08 | WEEK 8: GOD'S FAVOR DOESN'T MAKE SENSE

1. John Goldingay, *Genesis for Everyone, Part 2: Chapters 17-50*, The Old Testament for Everyone, (Louisville, Westminster John Knox Press: 2010).
2. David Guzik, *Genesis*, Enduring Word Commentary Series, (Goleta: Enduring Word Media, 2018).

09 | WEEK 9: GOD BRINGS US TOGETHER

1. John Goldingay, *Genesis for Everyone, Part 2: Chapters 17-50*, The Old Testament for Everyone, (Louisville, Westminster John Knox Press: 2010).

10 | WEEK 10: GOD ISN'T FINISHED YET

No sources this week, cuz we're smart like that.

START A DELIGHT

HELP US SPREAD THE WORD ABOUT DELIGHT!

There are thousands of college women all across the country that need Christ-centered community but have no idea Delight exists!!! We need women like you to help spread the word.

If this community has impacted your life in any way, don't you want to help other women experience it, too?

If you know a friend who loves Jesus and who would make an amazing Delight leader—tell her about Delight! With just a few texts you could indirectly reach hundreds of college women on another campus!

How cool is that?!

www.delightministries.com

Point them to our website where they can sign up to bring Delight to their campus! Once they sign up, they will hear from us and will get everything they need to make this community happen at their university.

So . . . send a couple texts, call a couple friends, maybe post about it on your socials, and let's reach a million more college women together!

DELIGHT DNA

You are officially family if you are holding this book in your hands! We want you to know who we are at Delight so you can truly feel like a part of the fam! You can scan this code below to explore our Delight DNA site, which was created for women just like you to understand more of our heartbeat as a ministry.

Within Delight DNA, Mac and Kenz share the story behind Delight and their vision for it as it continues to grow. We dive deeper into our Core Values and even share a five-day devo to help you incorporate them into your everyday life! We can't wait for you to check out this amazing resource and pray that it makes you feel connected to all of us here at Delight!

For more information, resources, or
encouragement head to . . .

WWW.DELIGHTMINISTRIES.COM